GRIEF MINISTRY
Helping Others Mourn

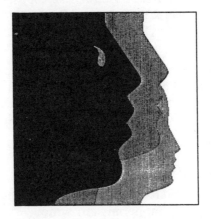

Donna Reilly Williams
and JoAnn Sturzl, PBVM

RESOURCE PUBLICATIONS, INC.
SAN JOSE, CALIFORNIA

Editorial director: Kenneth Guentert
Production editor: Kathi Drolet
Art director: Terri Ysseldyke-All
Production assistant: Elizabeth J. Asborno

Grateful acknowledgment is extended to those granting permission to reprint the following copyrighted material:

Excerpts from *The New Jerusalem Bible,* copyright © 1985 by Darton, Longman & Todd, Ltd. and Doubleday, a division of Bantam, Doubleday, Dell Publishing Group, Inc. Reprinted by permission.

That's Enough, page xiii, Copyright © 1988 Deanna Edwards. Used by permission of Rock Canyon Music Publishers, 777 E. Walnut, Provo, Utah, 84604.

Library of Congress Cataloging-in-Publication Data available.

5 4 3 2 1 / 94 93 92 91 90

*We dedicate this book, with love, to all who have shared
their journeys through the Valley of the Shadow,
from whom we have learned and grown;
and especially to Ed and Emily Robles,
Tommy and Edna Mae Carter,
Herb and Rita Connaughton,
Dick and Virginia Barth,
and Agnes and Robert Escobedo.*

Table of Contents

Foreword

Ranier Maria Rilke, the German poet laureate, makes the observation concerning death that there is a little death for each of us and a large death for most of us. The little death is the mere cessation of all biological human function: our heart stops beating, we stop breathing, and we are dead! The large death is a descriptive way of looking at the relentless process of our ongoing dying.

At each point in time, as we move from wellness to illness and on to terminal illness, we are faced with an ever-deepening existential need to make sense and meaning out of what is happening to us. For, as Jure Kristo has said:

> From an observation of how human beings live, grow, develop, deteriorate (even die), or flourish, one can detect that to be human is to create one's "worlds," to construct universes where disparate (and desperate) elements of experiences are integrated into wholes that provide one with a sense of purpose, order, manageability, orientation—in a word, with meaning.[1]

Fatal illness and final dying, each with its ultimate kinds of meaning, seem to require both special understanding and help with management. The person now becomes a dying patient. For whatever of life is left, the significant others who surround the patient face the difficult challenge of integrating into meaning all that is happening so inexorably.

Astute students of human nature observe that human beings are *homo poeta,* meaning-makers. Because most dying people have great difficulty making any significant meaning out of dying, there are other human beings, thank God, who make themselves available. By presence, space, care, and love, they help the dying to live while they die. Unfortunately, there are not many human beings who have either the desire or the ability to help.

Donna Williams and JoAnn Sturzl, PBVM, have sensed the great need to identify and train gifted and concerned persons to help give meaning to dying persons and their loved ones.

The beauty and strength of the book you are about to read (and hopefully use) is to be found in the careful way the authors have brought together knowledge, values, attitudes, and skills for caring for the dying that are quite complete, succinct, and educationally exciting.

Prayerfully, it is hoped that this book will have wide reading, be used in training many caregivers, and at last, come to the meaningful comfort of those who might otherwise die virtually alone and without meaning—the worst kind of death!

Wil Alexander
Professor of Clinical Ministry
Loma Linda University
Loma Linda, California

Acknowledgments

The authors of *Grief Ministry* wish first, to thank God for a friendship that has borne fruit in this work. Our loving gratitude goes out also to those who helped us in our own journeys to wholeness: Donna says, "Thanks," to Aldona Ewazko, SCSL, Rev. Dr. William Schmidt, and Rev. Kenneth Hayden. "There is something of each of you in who I am and what I write." JoAnn thanks Mary Ann Connell, SNJM, "for leading me to a deeper relationship with myself, God, and others."

This book could not have happened without the loving support of our families and colleagues and the direct contributions of Dr. Nancy Reeves, Deanna Edwards, Marilyn Boyington, and Rabbi Jonathan Brown. Rita Connaughton and Beverly Franco shared their secretarial gifts. Brother Edward Smink, OH, Dr. Linda Harper, Virginia Barth, Dr. Wilbur Alexander, and Dr. Nancy Reeves read, edited, and shared wisdom with us.

Through the communal effort of preparing this, our gift, we have come to recognize our wealth in those we love.

I can't remove your loneliness
Or heal your broken heart.
Can't take away the shadows
That make your night so dark,
But I can stay beside you
When life is getting tough.
If we come close together, that's enough.

I don't have all the answers
And I don't know what to say.
I can't bring you the sunshine
Or take the rain away,
But I can always hold you
When the storm is getting rough.
If we come close together, that's enough.

I had to learn so many things
And fail so many times
Before the day I finally realized
If we could take the sorrow
From every loss that comes along
We'd have to take the loving out of life!

I can't remove the dangers
From a world so full of fears.
I can't make living safer
Or take away your tears.
But I can always love you
With a love that you can trust.
And if we come close together, that's enough.

Deanna Edwards
That's Enough

Introduction

One of the most basic calls in the Judeo-Christian faith tradition is the call to minister to hurting members of the community.God does not want human beings to be alone; that is why the people of Israel were called to become a nation, and that is why Jesus asks his followers to work for unity. Traditionally, places of worship have been centers of sanctuary and support. In the Bible, childless Hannah went to the temple to petition God to grant the desire of her heart (1 Sam 1:7-11). The psalmist reflects on God's temple, "Even the sparrow has found a home, the swallow a nest to place its young: your altars, Yahweh Sabaoth, my King and my God" (Ps 84:3).

God has always commanded that we respond to the pain around us.

> *Is not this the sort of fast that pleases me: to break unjust fetters, to undo the thongs of the yoke, to let the oppressed go free, and to break all yokes? Is it not sharing your food with the hungry, and sheltering the homeless poor; if you see someone lacking clothes, to clothe him, and not to turn away from your own kin? Then your light will blaze out like the dawn and your wound be quickly healed over. Saving justice for you will go ahead and Yahweh's glory come behind you (Is 58:6-8).*

1

Jesus carried on the tradition of ministry when he instructed his followers to "cure the sick, raise the dead, cleanse those suffering from virulent skin-diseases, drive out devils. You received without charge, give without charge" (Mt 10:8).

In the Middle Ages, Christian monks and nuns nursed plague victims and crusaders and provided safe hostels for travelers. Through the centuries, people of faith have reached out to lepers and other outcasts of society. Still today, people regard churches and temples as places where their needs will be addressed.

Traditionally, those with some official public commitment—the ordained or vowed—have reached out in this sort of ministry. Whether they were appropriately trained or not, they were expected to accept ministry to the suffering as a large part of the mandate. Today, however, the traditional structures are disappearing and God seems to be calling lay believers to respond. Some people rationalize that lay ministers are needed to fill in for the current lack of clerical vocations; but the reality is that every Christian and every Jew is mandated by God to care for others. We believe that God is simply asking us to accept that vocation.

Working together in a large urban parish, we, the authors, became aware of the acute need for preparation programs for those who were responding to the ministerial call. Dealing with death and dying fills most people with fear and feelings of inadequacy.

There are two major reasons for the fear. First, dealing with others' dying and grieving is also a confrontation with personal mortality. Second, most people do not understand the experiences of those who are dying and mourning, and so are afraid that they will "do the wrong thing" and possibly make the mourning person's experience even more painful.

Having come to understand these aspects of fear, we decided to design a program of preparation for those who felt called to these frightening ministries. This book is the outgrowth of that preparation. It will teach you not only how to help others, but also how to better understand yourself as you pass through normal, though painful, life transitions. The companion *Facilitator's Manual* is designed for use by those who teach both grief dynamics and ministry to the bereaved. [1]

Loss is a part of every life change. When a loss happens, the natural reaction is to attempt to re-establish emotional equilibrium by gradually redefining the parameters of a new life phase. We realize that for many the concept that we grieve for many losses throughout life will be new. But it is an important concept to understand in this fast-paced world, where change, transition, is the norm rather than the exception. Hopefully, through this book you will come to understand this concept and learn to recognize and care for many types of grief-pain in yourself and in others.

Caregivers who encourage people to approach death and other losses in meaningful ways also embark on a voyage of personal self-discovery. It is a powerful experience to respond to the same challenge you present to the other, to attempt to incarnate and embody the same truths you impart.

The faith and prayer dimensions are foundations for the grieving process. Confrontation with death puts one in touch with the reality and limitations of human mortality. It challenges one to ask the questions that we believe can best be answered through the reality of God's healing love for humanity. Scripture and prayer reflection help to focus thoughts and feelings, reassure us of God's promises, and give occasion to talk with and listen to God. We believe the reality of death can lead human beings to an awareness of a need for God and others.

A story that illustrates human beings confronting questions about death and its meaning is found in Chaim Potok's book, *My Name Is Asher Lev*. Asher, a recognized artist, recalls a boyhood talk he had with his father, whom he had found looking at a bird lying against the curb near their house.

"Is it dead, Papa?" I was six and I could not bring myself to look at it.

"Yes," I heard him say in a sad and distant way.
"Why did it die?"
"Everything that lives must die."
"Everything? You too, Papa? And Mama?"
"Yes."
"And me?"
"Yes," he said. Then he added in Yiddish, "but may it be only after you live a long and good life, my Asher."
I could not grasp it. I forced myself to look at the bird. Everything alive would one day be as still as that bird?
"Why?" I asked.
"That's the way the Ribbono Shel Olem made the world, Asher."
"Why?"
"So life would be more precious, Asher. Something that is yours forever is not precious."[2]

In such a manner, human persons walk and talk with each other and with God, living the questions and letting the questions lead to transformation and growth. No one can remove another's pain, but almost everyone can walk beside and support another who is sorrowful.

It is also possible to receive from those who grieve. They can teach the reality of darkness and light, death and resurrection. People in mourning often see life from a new vantage point. Suffering can transform values and understandings. For those who journey with others in grief, who stand in the mysterious privilege of being called to comfort, there can come an understanding of Jesus' beatitude:

"Blessed are those who mourn:
they shall be comforted" (Mt 5:4).

The following quotation illustrates this growth and is a favorite of ours. The author is a parent who learned how to find new richness in life through the pain of loss.

I don't know why.
I'll never know why.

I don't have to know why.
I don't like it.
I don't have to like it.
What I do have to do is make a choice about my living.
What I do want to do is accept and go on living.
The choice is mine.
I can go on living,
valuing every moment in a way I never did before,
or I can be destroyed by it, and in turn destroy others.
I thought I was immortal.
That my family and children were also.
That tragedy happened only to others.
But I know now that life is tenuous and valuable.
So I am choosing to go on living,
making the most of the time I have,
valuing my family and friends,
in a way never before possible.[3]

We find it interesting to see who God sends to become part of these training programs. Each person adds a special dimension to the group. The first time we presented the material of this book, a man came who was undergoing chemotherapy for cancer. Six months later he died. Something about his presence in the group, about his life and death struggle, had been a gift to all of us. Although we had pre-planned the contents of the sessions, we could never have planned for the tremendous change and learning we all experienced from his presence with us, his life, and his dying.

In addition to participants' growth in skills and confidence for accomplishing difficult ministry, many express a change in their faith and life values. One woman said, "My values have changed. Material things aren't important to me anymore." Many express joy at their growing ability to reach out to neighbors and co- workers at times of loss or death.

This change or conversion that people experience seems comparable to what Laurie and Joseph Braga describe in their forward to Elizabeth Kubler-Ross' book, *Death, The Final Stage of Growth*:

> All that you are and all that you've been and done is cul-
> minated in your death. When you're dying, if you're fortunate
> enough to have some prior warning (other than that we have
> all the time if we come to terms with our finiteness), you get
> your final chance to grow, to become more truly who you are,
> to become more fully human. But you don't need to, nor
> should you, wait until death is at your doorstep before you
> start to really live. If you can begin to see death as an invisible,
> but friendly, companion on your life's journey—gently
> reminding you not to wait til tomorrow to do what you need
> to do—then you can learn to *live* your life rather than simply
> passing through it.[4]

Grief Ministry discusses the general aspects of grieving: empathy, communication, listening, and prayer. It also looks at
some specific losses such as the death of a baby and suicide. In
writing about grief, we emphasize that mourning is not limited
to the death experience but occurs at all life transitions: divorce,
amputation, even high school graduation. "Most of us are living
through grief or grieving through life most of the time, for life
is conditioned by small and significant daily losses."[5]

Chapter One

Gifted, Called, and Sent

Indeed, from his fullness we have, all of us,
received (Jn 1:16).

Most people have joyful memories of receiving a gift from someone who loves them. Because a gift is an expression of the affection of the person who has given it, it carries a twofold meaning: enjoyment of the gift itself as well as satisfaction and inner joy, because this gift is a symbol of love from the giver. Much later, one can reflect upon and savor the love that the gift represents.

When selecting a gift for a loved one, people generally choose carefully and select what is special, what is "just right" for this person. Often the people are known so well that it is not necessary to ask them what they would like to have. There is a "heart knowledge" of the person, and it is out of this oneness of heart that the giver ponders and selects the right gift.

God is the ultimate lover and gift-giver, expressing love through the beauties of the world, especially in the creation of humanity in the Holy image. Salvation history is the story of God's limitless love, first in the creation of the world out of

God's wish to share life, and then in the creation of human persons, with whom wisdom is shared.

> *I have loved you with an everlasting love (Jer 31:3).*

> *Do not be afraid, for I am with you (Is 43:5).*

> *On the day that God created Adam*
> *he made him in the likeness of God.*
> *Male and female he created them (Gen 5:2).*

> *For Yahweh himself is the giver of wisdom, from his*
> *mouth issue knowledge and understanding (Prov 2:6).*

Christians find in Jesus—God's ultimate gift—God in the flesh, incarnate in humanity. Through Jesus, Christians find complete unity with God. Before his death and resurrection, Jesus promised that he would not leave his followers alone.

> *"I shall ask the Father,*
> *and he will give you another Paraclete*
> *to be with you for ever, the Spirit of truth" (Jn 14:16).*

Christians believe that the Holy Spirit is given to the faithful, who can experience the Spirit's gifts in their lives. "The fruit of the Spirit is love, joy, peace, patience, kindness, goodness, trustfulness, gentleness and self-control" (Gal 5:22).

THE GIFTS OF MINISTRY

> *There are many different gifts, but it is always the same spirit; there are different ways of serving, but it is always the same Lord. There are many different forms of activity, but in everybody it is the same God who is at work in them all (1 Cor 12:4-6).*

Every believer has been given unique gifts for ministry. Even if the gift seems the same as someone else's, it is not the same because each person is a unique individual; thus the ways the gift is experienced and expressed will differ. People should never belittle their personal gifts and talents just because they seem common or unimportant. Some gifts are needed in many situations, so the Lord has endowed many ministers with those particular talents. Other gifts are needed only in special circumstances, so only a few persons are endowed with those gifts. For example, the need for grief therapists or surgeons is not as widespread, therefore, fewer people have these gifts.

Some people deny their gifts for ministry from a sense of false humility. They can have the mistaken notion that to receive praise for good qualities leads to pride. This prevents them from recognizing and affirming God's goodness, and then the talents are hidden. Many ancient prophets tried to persuade God not to use their gifts (Jer 1:1-10), but God always persevered and helped them to believe in themselves. Jesus also encouraged his followers:

> *No one lights a lamp and puts it in some hidden place or under a tub (Lk 11:33).*

Real humility acknowledges the truth, and the truth is that God has blessed each person with unique gifts. One response is to praise and thank God and to make use of these gifts in service to others.

Another reason many people hide their talents is that they do not feel "holy enough." They have the idea that any person who ministers in the name of the Lord must be a perfect person. If this were the case, God would have no hands on this earth. We, the authors, have never met a perfect person. Although we are both women who work full-time in pastoral ministry, we are far from perfect. With faith, hope, and trust, we accept that the work of God is being accomplished in us, and we struggle every day to accept God's forgiveness and to love ourselves, always remembering who is the core and source of the work we do.

The most effective caregivers are usually those who realize how far from perfection they are and how much they need God's help and inspiration. Out of this awareness, a person can approach broken people as someone who will understand and not judge; this sort of rapport encourages the struggle toward wholeness and healing.

It is not necessary to completely sort out every personal problem before beginning to minister. When we ourselves get nervous about the responsibility of our call, we remember other leaders and prophets who were called, in their woundedness, by God. Moses threw out every excuse he could think of for not leading the people of God to freedom (Ex 4:1-17). But God had an answer for every problem and gave Moses support for each task he faced. Jonah tried to run away from God (Jon 1:3), and Jeremiah thought that he was too young to speak for the Lord (Jer 1:1-10). When Esther approached the king, her husband, to beg for her people's life, Scripture tells us that her heart "shrank with fear" (Est 5:5), but because she asked God's support and believed that she was doing God's will, she persevered and Israel was saved.

It is wonderful to know that God finds goodness in all people, abilities of which they may not even be aware. These abilities are pure gifts (grace) from God. Like Moses and the others who followed him through the pages of Scripture, God will support all who are willing to trust.

MINISTRY DISCERNMENT

Often, programs for ministry discernment begin by identifying needs. We believe that the starting point for discernment should be the unique gifts that God has given to members of the community rather than the community's needs. This starting point implies a trust that all the gifts needed to bring about God's reign will indeed be given.

In order to listen to God and to identify the particular ministry to which you are being called, it is important to be aware of and claim your God-given gifts. If you can minister out of these gifts, you will be living the unique identity that God has given you. The more faithful you are to being the person that God created you to be, the more happy and satisfied you will be, and the more life you will have to share with others.

You will come to know the truth, and the truth will set you free(Jn 8:32).

One sign that you are living your personal truth and exercising your God-given talents is through a feeling of enlivenment and creativity; you will experience a dynamic and peaceful sense of living your best self.

Once people begin to touch their inner depth, they are able to awaken others in their depths and help them discover their own inner resources. André Rochais calls this a "creational gaze."[1] He explains this term in reference to God the Creator, who brings human beings into existence by the power of the creative gaze. Faith-filled caregivers come to others in God's name to be mediators of God's presence, by reason of

...this God who has faith in them because he knows what they have been created with, and the growth dynamism he placed within them.[2]

IDENTIFYING YOUR GIFTS AND TALENTS

How do you identify your gifts and talents? How do you help others identify and claim theirs? You must begin by looking within.

The following suggestions are based on the value system of *Personality and Human Relations*.[3] These steps can be helpful in discerning giftedness.

1. Reflect on what things are natural and effortless for you. Sometimes, people will point out a quality or talent that they see in you, and you may minimize it as a talent because it seems so natural. We all have aspects of ourselves like this. Make a list of your natural and effortless activities.

2. Ask yourself, "What positive qualities do other people affirm in me?" Reflect on those people who know you well and to whom you feel close. Make a list of the positive qualities they affirm in you.

3. Think of people to whom you are attracted and who make you feel more alive because of their lives, their words, their works, or because of what they do to help you become yourself. Ask yourself, "What positive aspects or talents in me did I become aware of through my contacts with these people?"

4. Every person is involved in various projects and activities. Some of these are done in a rather routine manner, with little awareness or sense that this activity has meaning or life. Other activities bring life, happiness, and satisfaction. Particular qualities or talents surface, and people feel that they are being their truest selves. Ask yourself, "What special qualities come to life in me through these activities?"

5. This method will enjoyably exercise your imagination. Ask yourself, "If I had the opportunity to do whatever I felt most deeply from within, what would I do

   a. that would give me satisfaction and happiness?"
   b. that would give my life a sense of meaning?"

c. that would allow me the possibility to give
of my best self?"

Allow yourself to imagine this dream, even if it seems wild. Then ask yourself, "What qualities or aspects of myself would this bring alive?"

If you enter deeply into an experience of any or all of the above reflections, then you might possibly come to a deeper knowledge of your gifts and talents. Try writing your responses to these reflections, as writing can sometimes help to move thoughts to a deeper level inside yourself.

YOUR RESPONSE

As you become more deeply aware of the gifts and positive qualities that God has given you, you can choose to respond to a call that allows those gifts to flourish. Ask God to help you discover how to use your gifts wisely and reverently. You may need to try a certain type of service for a while, to experience it and determine whether or not it is right for you.

One way to strengthen an awareness of your gift is to occasionally spend some time in quiet, prayerful reflection on the lived experience of your service. The following simple reflection from *Ministry Reflection and Assessment* may be helpful.

1. Begin with a prayer.
2. Recall a recent time when you were helping another. Which qualities of your inner self were alive? What gift or gifts were especially manifested in you?
3. How did God touch another with your gift(s)?
4. In what ways can you foster the growth of this gift within yourself?
5. Can you recall some Scripture passage that validates this gift?[4]

Write your reflections. It is best to reflect on these questions with a small group and share what you have written because the focus will be on your *gift* and how it touches others, rather than on your activity.

BEING VERSUS DOING

There is a difference between service to others that flows from your inner self and unique gifts, and service that is merely focused on doing a task. When your ministry comes from your unique identity, you are engaged at a deeper level, and you bring more of your real self to the other. You may find that you have more energy to serve others because you are not pushing and straining to be and do something that is not truly who you are. You are likely to feel more trusting of yourself and of God's presence both in you and in the other person. When your caring for another comes from your inner depths (the being part of yourself), you are more likely to enable people to reach into their depths and discover their own resources and inner life.

On the other hand, when you reach out to others from your need for doing, it probably makes you feel good. You have a feeling of accomplishment. But when caregivers act *only* out of a personal need to "do something," to feel good, to make a difference, it is less effective than ministering out of "being." The difference between a care-giver and a caring giver is a subtle one. Although you may physically do the same things whether you *be* or *do*, the quality and effects will be considerably richer if you act out of your inner self.

Chapter Two

Death in Our Society

I (D.R.W.) was a patient in an African hospital when a young man died in the next room. Although I had heard about the local custom of mourning, my North American mind had not really understood what would happen.

Although this was a government hospital in the middle of a city, the drums began to beat in the hospital courtyard, and slowly, the people gathered. About an hour later, a pickup truck brought the village family to the hospital. Everyone filed into the hospital ward and gathered around the bed of the dead man. I was told that in the old days, at this point there would have been great wailing and keening; but for this man, the people sang hymns. Many of them were familiar tunes with African words, sung with the wondrous harmony common to African music.

Nothing really surprised me as yet, and I wandered back to my own room, expecting that the mourners would soon finish their ritual and be on their way. But they did not leave. For over four hours they sang and prayed. They passed bowls of food and cups of drink, and one time when I peeked in, the group looked more like a party than a wake. And always the beautiful hymns continued. The young man's body was uncovered, and a woman (I was told she was his mother) lovingly stroked his arms and legs and then clasped him to her breast, tears streaming down

15

her face. Finally, she released him. A wooden door was brought, and gently the men lifted the body and placed it, covered with a sheet, onto the door. Raising him above their heads, they carried him out to the back of the pickup truck for his journey to the village. Looking out, it seemed as if most of the villagers had gathered at the hospital. But I knew from past experience that these were people who lived in the city. Because of lack of transportation, they would not be able to travel to a village in time for the burial (that would take place in the evening).

In Africa, bodies must be buried quickly due to the heat. And since there are very few clerical people, most burials are the task of the villagers. I was in one village where there were three burials in one day (which is not unusual). In Africa the average life span is thirty-nine years and death is a reality of life.

Working in North American hospitals, I have often reflected upon that African experience. Many times I have spoken to the families of someone who has just died. The conversation may be with a single person who has remained at the hospital, or it may be by telephone. It usually goes something like this.

"Mr. Jones, Dr. Brown has asked me to call and tell you that your brother has died, about five minutes ago."

(Long pause) "Oh. So it's over. Well, what comes next? What do we do now?"

"Would you or someone in your family like to come to the hospital? I can ask the nurses to keep John in the room until you arrive."

"Well...do we need to come? I mean, is there something we need to sign? I already told the doctor that he could do an autopsy. Do we need to be there?"

"No, there is no legal reason why you need to come. You can call in to the office in the morning and tell them which mortuary you have chosen.

"Are you sure that nobody in your family wants to spend some last time with John's body. There's no hurry to move him for a couple of hours."

"No, that's OK. We'll call in the morning."

This type of conversation always makes me sad. Of course, the dead person doesn't care whether his or her family comes to the hospital. What makes me sad is that this conversation is the beginning of a funeral ritual that is comprised of one part grieving and three parts denial.

By contrast, the ritual around the bed of the young African man had been so natural, so healthy. Those people experienced death on a regular basis, and they knew it was painful. They also knew that they had to acknowledge it and share their pain if they were to survive. The hospital staff did all they could to facilitate their ritual; although patients were sleeping on the floor, the staff did not rush to move the body until the mourners were ready. The ritual after a death was as much a part of hospital routine as were the lifesaving procedures in which they were trained. Nobody thought to close the door of the ward to prevent nosy North Americans from looking in. And even if they had wished to move the dying man to a private room, there was no such place in the hospital.

A couple of generations ago, North Americans usually died at home. They often died in bed with the family gathered around

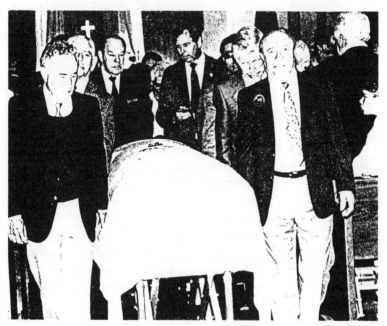

them. The family had the task of preparing the body for burial. Usually the wake was held in the family parlor or main room of the house. Now, one of the requests we often hear from dying patients is "Please don't let me die alone." What a sad commentary on our society! We deny the greatest realities of life, and hand in hand with this denial comes an abhorrence for any talk of death and finality.

LEARNING TO DENY

The way a society responds to death is related to the way that society responds to other major transitions and changes that are normal to the lives of its people. Similarly, individuals will respond to major losses in ways they have learned to respond to other life transitions. If a person has habitually responded to change with anger, that person will likely display a great deal of anger when confronted with death. The flexible person will likely approach death more gracefully and with more acceptance.

Contemporary industrial society fosters the notion that all advancement in life quality must nurture happiness. Unfortunately, some transitions cannot come about without pain. Our contemporary society does not provide the ritual means (often provided by traditional societies) to express that pain. Today many people are taught to pretend that pain does not exist, and when it is impossible to avoid the pain, society invents ways to pretend that all is well.

Think about the statement often made to a child whose pet has died: "Never mind, we can get a new puppy." Often couples who have lost a baby hear something similar: "Never mind. You are young and you can have other babies." Even the widowed are told, "Well, before long you will feel like marrying again." As for divorce, many people just pretend the marriage never happened, and many remarry on the day the divorce becomes final. Children who haven't yet learned to push away the pain can be chastised for not accepting their parents' quick remarriage.

Most people do not like to acknowledge endings. Society has developed supreme denial skills. Many times Christian churches reflect this with the offer of heaven without the challenge to "take up my cross."

When death can no longer be pushed away and denied, a hospitalized dying person is often placed in a single, darkened room. The door is closed on the pretext of giving privacy to the family, although often there is no family. Hospital staff tiptoe past that room, avoiding it unless they must enter for duty. The clergyperson appears, recites some quick prayers, shakes the hands of family members, and disappears with a shake of the head and an "I'm sorry." The auntie who begins to weep too loudly is quickly silenced by her children: "Come on, mother. Don't get yourself into a state." There are requests for sedatives for senior grievers, and the doctors comply. And when nothing further can be done to ward off death, the family will leave, the halls will be cleared, and the body will be spirited away in an ingenious device that looks like an empty stretcher, just in case someone sees that a death has occurred in a hospital. The next time the family sees the body, it will be laid out in a "slumber room" at the local mortuary.

Learning to deny loss is a process that occurs as human beings grow up. When a small child is unhappy, he cries. The baby who is left with a sitter and is unsure that her parents will return shrieks out in fear. The little one left for the first day of nursery school or kindergarten will cling to his parents. The adolescent leaving the safety of elementary school approaches the larger world of junior high with excitement mixed with a natural fear of the unknown.

Adolescents' transitions are recognized as painful, sometimes terrifying. Parents, teachers, and others try to smooth this away and make these years into happy ones. This is not wrong, but sometimes it is taken to such an extreme that the realistic fears are not validated. Adolescents are usually taught instead that they must face life with courage and a smile.

Traditional cultures are often healthier in their transition rituals. They designed their rituals to test the adolescents' readiness to take on the joys *and* the pains of adult life. The components of the rituals illustrated both of these aspects of life. Traditional rituals often physically mutilate children in order to symbolize transition. We don't have to go this far, but we do have to somehow develop the ability to acknowledge, not deny, our children's fears and to emphasize to them that a life that holds pain is still a good life. Pain and joy must be allowed to weave the complete tapestry, or else we deny the full human experience. We must develop rituals of transition which illustrate this fullness.

RETURN TO HEALTH

The pendulum always swings. Human persons will almost always, in the end, respond to the call to wholeness that is incarnate within them.

From our perspective, it seems that in the last twenty years many people are gradually realizing an emptiness in life (despite efforts for constant fulfillment). Many see that nothing can fill the interior void until the whole reality of life and death is faced. Churches and temples have reflected this by their move away from distant, meaningless funeral services and toward attempts to involve the mourners themselves in the services, even in the planning stages. Many now have professional grief counselors on staff. Most worship communities have members of the congregation who visit hospitals and support grieving families.

Universities and seminaries offer courses to help people understand the grief experience, and these classes are usually very popular. People flock to places where they can speak of their pain because they realize that these conversations will help them become more whole and will ease some of the loneliness of living in a society that worships only the strong and the beautiful.

One of the most exciting developments is the *palliative care* or hospice movement. Palliative care simply means that, for a person who is dying, the only aggressive treatment that will be undertaken is to increase the level of physical, emotional, or spiritual comfort. No effort is made to deny death or prolong life. The hospice creates an atmosphere of acceptance, with trained professionals who facilitate the necessary conversations and questions about death. These people realize that some of the questions will not have answers, and they reassure the dying person and loved ones that this is natural and good. It is all right to be grieving. The staff breaks down taboos about death, and they avoid euphemisms. They acknowledge pain and anger, and they validate feelings, all of which then become bridges for growth toward inner harmony.

Hospice physicians are now becoming involved in teaching medical students and health personnel about death and dying. Generally, medical students have been taught the pathophysiology of dying but not its psychosocial and spiritual aspects. Many physicians are aware of this lack. They often possess qualities of caring and compassion but have been trained to defeat death, not to accept it. What appears to be indifference and emotional distance in physicians may be a self-protective insulation against death and their feelings toward the dying person.

One hospice physician involved in teaching medical students about death and dying uses storytelling, experiential exercises, and group sharing. He wants to be a role model for his students, so he allows them to see that he experiences confusion and helplessness in the face of death because he is human. He believes that physicians who are able to confront both their own and the dying person's fears about death have a unique opportunity to improve the quality of life.[1]

There is still a long way to go and a great deal of education is needed before most of society accepts the reality that there is a delicate balance between prolonging life and allowing persons to move gracefully toward death.

Chapter Three

The Question of Control

When we teach, we often tell our students that if they only remember one word we speak, let it be the word *control*. Understanding this word and the concept underlying it can make a tremendous difference in understanding the agony of the aging and ill.

It is important to understand that there are two aspects of control: the personal loss of control over one's own life and, as caregivers, the powerful temptation to abuse control. This abuse includes making arbitrary decisions about the ill or aging person's care, without dialogue with that person.

From the day of birth human persons try to accomplish control. During childhood parents urge children to learn to control their tempers, speech habits, public behavior, bodily functions. Children start school, only to learn that they must master a whole new set of self-controls. In the teen years adolescents struggle to wrest control of many life experiences from the hands of their parents and other adults. Finally, young adults rejoice in their newfound freedom and control of their own lives.

Soon, however, adults realize that many factors, including personal decisions, control the course of their lives. Then the areas where adults *do* maintain independence become even more precious. All human beings need to believe that they are in control of themselves, their personal actions, and decisions. That belief makes a person feel strong and whole. Much of psychological therapy aims at restoring a lost sense of selfhood and strength .

LOSS OF CONTROL DUE TO AGING

It is impossible however, to prevent the inevitable changes that happen with time. Bodies lose their flexibility and strength. Sometimes even the brain is attacked by illness, limiting mental agility. Gradually the older generation is forced to give up much of the coveted control, and the younger generation takes over. Children become caregivers to their parents; roles are reversed.

This is a humiliating, frustrating reality, and the fact that it happens to so many will not make it any easier when it is experienced personally. A widow who moves into a small room in her daughter's house, the older couple confined to a bed or a wheelchair in a convalescent home, the widower struggling to maintain the family home—all feel terribly frustrated. They can no longer function as they used to. Much of their self-identity was tied in with their ability to function, and now they begin to lose sight of themselves. To make matters worse, *ageism* reminds them over and over that persons of their age are without value. They often do not have great financial freedom, and their employers tell them they are too old to function constructively. Magazines they read glorify youth. Many people with whom they recreated are gone. They attend more funerals than any other social event. Often, failing health restricts their mobility. Many lose their driver's licenses.

Who has not been frustrated with an elderly driver who pulls in front of a car without looking or who holds up traffic by driving below the speed limit? Who has not thought, "That person should not be driving"? The next time this happens, it might be helpful to remember that although some old people should not drive because of failing sight or another diminished physical ability, they are sometimes clinging to their ability to drive as their only contact with the world outside their homes. In other words, this may be the only remaining area of control over their own lives. For younger, healthy people,it may seem simple: If they are not safe, get them off the road. But to them, it is not that simple, and they will fight to maintain their independence, sometimes even driving without a license after the state has revoked it. While driving illegally is wrong, the pain of these people can also be touching.

You might be asked to visit in the home of an older person with a reputation for being cranky or even downright nasty. Granted, some crabby old people were crabby young people. Often though, frustrated old people who feel isolated and devalued are fighting back at a world that treats them poorly. These are frequently people who once derived a great deal of self-worth from what they did, from their personal competence. They have not learned to appreciate their inner worth and resources. They don't know how to smell the roses or take delight in the smile of a grandchild.

Mrs. Fields had a reputation in the nursing home. She was in a private room because nobody wanted to live with her. She had raised eight children, and these adult children told us that she had been a wonderful mother who had completely looked after their needs and had kept the home immaculate. Every Sunday, her family, rubbed and scrubbed, had been displayed at the local Baptist church, and she had derived great pleasure from the compliments she received on her beautiful family. She had worked with the women's group at the church, and every Christmas her pies were the first to sell at the annual bake sale.

Her husband had run the local stationery shop, and although they were never very close, she was just the wife he needed because her being "Superwife" freed him to pursue his business and civic interests. All in all, she had built for herself exactly the life she had always wanted.

But one by one, Mrs. Fields' children grew up. The girls built their own lives, but they continued to visit as often as possible.

They still loved it when Mrs. Fields called and told them she had baked a pie for them to pick up and take to their families. One son was killed in a war, and another moved far away. He phoned every week, and sometimes he came home for Christmas. The youngest son, Jeff, completely defied and humiliated his parents by becoming a Catholic priest.

Then one morning, Mrs. Fields woke up to find that she could not move or speak. Her daughter found her in bed at three in the afternoon and "shipped me to the hospital" from where she was transferred directly to the nursing home.

Now she was "Mabel," even to the young girl who brought the food tray. She was wakened at a certain time each day, washed, placed in a wheelchair, and wheeled to sit in front of a television to watch inane game shows all morning. People told her what to eat, when to sleep, what to wear, even when to go to the bathroom. Most of the time, she didn't speak; when she did, the words she spoke shocked ever herself, and then she would feel terribly ashamed for several hours.

She could no longer bake for her family or even talk to her grandchildren. When they came to visit, the adults sat in front of her and looked embarrassed because they couldn't think of what to say. The children ran around and bothered the other residents, and the teen-agers whined things like, "Can we go now?" to their parents.

Mrs. Fields lived for seven years in the nursing home before I (D.R.W.) met her. After a few days, I realized that she must be frustrated. She had built her life around being needed by others, and now nobody needed her. She had earned a place of respect in the town. Now everyone called her "Mabel," a name only her intimate friends and family had used before her stroke.

My first step toward giving her back control was to call her "Mrs. Fields" and acknowledge what I thought must be some of her frustration. I sat beside her and told her that I had heard that she was a wonderful mother and that I imagined it must hurt a lot not to be able to do things for her children anymore. This lady, who for seven years had never shown emotion except to utter blasphemies, began to cry. She was obviously embarrassed, so I reached out and took her in my arms, assuring her that her tears were perfectly normal. After she had cried, she said, "Don't know." Those two words contained all the meaning of her life. They opened the path for us to communicate about all the changes and hurts she had experienced. As the days passed, she led me through her loneliness, very slowly but very clearly.

The staff in the nursing home said that, for the first few days, Mrs. Fields seemed sad and depressed. But about five days of our sharing, she suddenly began to eat more and even to say a word or two when she wanted some special food from the table. Gradually, over the next weeks, she began to smile at the other residents. After about a month, she took an interest in some crafts, and the therapist was able to help her form some Christmas ornaments for her children.

Mrs. Fields eventually died. She never became too socially outgoing and always preferred to live in a private room. But she had become a more peaceful woman because her family and the professional caregivers learned to acknowledge the reality of her life and to include her in their lives. Her children no longer sat in embarrassed silence; they began to tell her all about their lives, their worries and joys. They brought photographs and mementos of special occasions. They told her how much they missed her, and they brought pies, which she had taught them how to bake, to share with the other residents. Mrs. Fields felt needed and respected again, and her life had meaning.

LOSS OF CONTROL DUE TO ILLNESS

People who are ill experience much the same frustration as those who are stripped of control due to age. Sick people are often confined to a bed in one room. Their families go on about their lives, dropping in to visit when they are able. Often sick people feel like both physical and financial burdens for their families. Sometimes businesses and incomes are lost. If the sickness leads to hospitalization, strangers are suddenly walking in and out of a sick person's room without knocking or introducing themselves.

Often sick people have both their bodies and psyches violated. The regular doctor might invite another to consult, without first asking the patient's permission. Generally sick people are afraid to question procedure or hospital etiquette for fear they will be labeled "uncooperative." Different doctors will give differing reports and prognoses; sometimes, those prognoses are delivered in a cool, seemingly uncaring manner. Strange, often frightening, words, sounds, smells, and food contribute to a sense of unreality, like a bad dream. But this is reality and for some, this will be the last reality of their lives.

Unfortunately, hospitals are usually large institutions, and it is difficult to run large institutions in such a way that newcomers feel personally touched by caregivers. Especially today, with chronic budget cuts and staff shortages, hospital caregivers find themselves frustrated in their attempts to spend quality time with many patients. The sick person may have a fear or concern but never have a chance to articulate this to a caregiver. The result is that both the caregivers and the patients feel isolated and depersonalized.

Many nursing and medical schools are now developing segments of their programs that help students learn how to give the "personal touch" within the constraints of modern care. These skills include learning how to listen better (so that the ill person will really be able to communicate concerns) and learning to better communicate diagnoses and treatment information (so that the patient feels included in all decisions).

Shortly before Christmas, Jim found out that he had terminal cancer. By Easter he was hospitalized for what everyone knew would be the last time. The hospital staff had become fond of Jim, and it was obvious from the number of caring friends who visited that he was a fine person.

Yet as his days ebbed away, Jim became more and more fussy and cross. He shouted at his son and told his grandson not to visit him again. He told his pastor that he wanted nothing to do with God.It seemed a terrible shame that this good man was wasting his last days and would leave so much pain in the hearts of those he loved.

It was natural that Jim was angry with the events of his life, especially his illness. It was understandable that since he was suffering from oxygen deprivation because of the state of his lungs, he might behave a bit irrationally. But this was not a man who would want to deliberately hurt his friends and family. Jim's pastor was an insightful professional and he expressed his concern to the hospital chaplain. We decided to find out if something else was bothering Jim.

I (D.R.W.) remember so clearly sitting quietly beside him and praying, watching his feeble lungs struggle to raise his chest for each breath. I remember his eyes opening and turning to me, then turning away—a soundless gesture that spoke volumes. I said, "Jim, you seem angry to see me here. Would you like me to leave?" (I was giving him control.)

"It really doesn't matter. There's always somebody here. I guess I'll be all alone soon enough."

"That sounds like a frightening thought. (Pause.) I think that I would feel frightened if I were lying in your place."

"Well...you might. (Long pause.) It's worse because I don't know what is happening."

"What does your doctor say?"

"She doesn't say anything to me. It seems like she talks to my kids, and they know, and then the nurses just come in and hook up some new medicine, or even blood...but nobody told me that it would be coming. Imagine that, they put someone else's blood into me, and they don't even ask me!"

"Wow! That must really confuse you and make you wonder about some things."

"It makes me mad. It makes me wonder if they think I'm already dead or something. I'm paying the doctor, but she talks to my son, not to me."

"Jim, would you feel a lot better if you thought people were consulting you about decisions for your care?"

"Of course I would. I'm not dead yet."

After reassuring him that I would try to establish better communication, I left Jim. That afternoon I met with his son who told me the doctor asked him not to tell his father the gravity of his illness because the shock would likely be too much for his weak heart. I assured the son that Jim knew he was dying, and together we went to see the doctor.

Dr. Reid seemed surprised when I told her that Jim was aware that he was dying. In medical school, she had been taught not to give patients this information because the knowledge could be too depressing. "Who told him?" she asked. I responded that I thought that anybody as sick as Jim could figure it out for himself. I also said that I thought Jim deserved to know the truth about himself and to be involved in treatment decisions. To her credit, the doctor listened and promised to speak directly with Jim that afternoon. She was a very competent, caring professional, but simply had not been introduced to contemporary theories about care of the dying.

The next day, I was pleased when I entered Jim's room. His son and grandson sat beside him, and he was resting with a smile on his face. They told me that when the doctor had come to visit, they had asked Jim's permission to be present and hear what she would say. Jim had readily agreed. He told the doctor that he wanted no more aggressive treatment. He wanted to be kept as comfortable as possible so that he could make amends with the people he had hurt, and could talk to God a few times before they met face to face. The doctor, very surprised, agreed, and the delighted family was reunited.

Although the above case study clearly illustrates a patient being helped to regain some control, it is important to remember that hospital personnel are not always so ready to listen to advice. While they do want the best for their patients, your insight as caregiver may contradict what they have previously learned and practiced. Always try to think of someone within the hospital structure, perhaps a doctor or social worker involved in palliative care, who will help you put forward the ill person's needs. Or if the patient is able, you might discuss the possibility of the sick person's stating his or her own needs to the medical staff.

Dr. Reid learned an important lesson from Jim about palliative care. Palliative care practiced in hospice units recognizes that persons are dying. It employs only medical procedures that will make dying more comfortable and meaningful. No attempt is made to prolong life, and, as much as possible, the sick people are encouraged to maintain control over decisions affecting their care. The philosophy is that death is yet another stage of life, which may be lived well or poorly. The caregivers attempt to encourage the sick to live their last days and hours as richly as possible.

Although most people do not die in acknowledged palliative care units, the principles of palliative care make sense for every dying person. The main tenets are honesty, support, and a willingness to give the person a sense of personal control for as long as possible.

Even if you are a lay minister with no official influence in the family or hospital's function, you are more important than you may think. You could be the only uninvolved person, the only one who can see with a clear eye what is happening.

CAREGIVING TO THE ILL

Whenever you sense an unhappiness in a person you are visiting ask yourself, "Is this at least partially a question of control? Is there any way in which I can help the person to regain any bit of that lost control?" Would you be able to arrange for a housebound person to get out once in a while, perhaps to worship or to a function with the community? If the person can't get out, could any of the functions be brought in? Some faith communities tape the worship services for the housebound to have and hear. Others distribute the flowers from services among the sick in the community.

Often, simply asking "What do you need?" will give you lots of clues about the hidden frustrations of the sick person. You may not be able to change things, but just listening and accepting frustration may help.

If the person is hospitalized, it is perfectly acceptable for you to speak with the nurse, chaplain, or social worker and share your concerns and perceptions. Do it in a positive manner and assume that the professional people involved also want the best for their patient. Identify yourself, telling them that you know you cannot make decisions for this person's care but that you would like to share your ideas to see what they think. Usually when you approach professional caregivers like this, they will at least give some consideration to your thoughts.

It is also appropriate for you or your pastor to speak with the sick person's family. In most cases, do this only after saying to the person something like, "Mary, I think that what you have told me is very important. May I have your permission to speak with your pastor and then one of us could help your husband understand your feelings?" The person may refuse; that is her right. Keep in mind that if a family has communicated poorly for many years, they might not ever change those patterns. This is not your fault. In such a case, all you can do is try to give support to the person to whom you were sent.

If you only learn one thing from this book, let it be this: Many, many frustrations of illness and aging are problems of loss of control. Any small return of that control often enables sick people to find some enjoyment in life. Through that enjoyment they can open their hearts to God, begin to accept their own reality, and move toward peace.

Chapter Four

The Dynamics of Grief

At the end of 1929, the level of suicide among adult men rose sharply. It continued to rise into 1930 and leveled off after that. What caused this terrible phenomenon? It seemed clear to everyone that the high suicide rate went hand in hand with the stock market crash. Highly successful businessmen could not face the pain of the loss of all their personal and financial investments. Those who jumped from buildings or shot themselves were the ones who could not muster the energy to begin again, to face a world without their self-definition (which had collapsed with the market on Wall Street).

Most people understand something about investment. If money or time is invested wisely, then a payoff is usually received sometime in the future. Even when buying a family home, people often hope to recover the investment, and perhaps even to make a profit. A young person is motivated to study hard by the thought that this study time is an investment for a future payoff of job security. When an investment is made and something personal is placed in someone else's hands, usually the investment can be drawn back. If someone cheats, absconds with the investment, the natural reaction is to feel betrayed and angry.

People also invest emotions. They give a part of their beings, their trust, to other people. Romantics say people give their hearts. This is not a bad analogy because the part offered to another person in an emotionally intimate relationship is something as vital to emotional well-being as the heart is to physical well-being.

As newborn infants, human beings begin to learn about emotional investment. Completely vulnerable, they nonetheless scream out and tell the world their needs. And, lo and behold, people come running to feed, clean, warm, and cuddle them. The people who respond most often and most positively, usually the parents, are the first people babies learn to trust. This involves more than response to physical needs. Infants who are kept warm, clean, and fed but who are not cuddled suffer from the syndrome called "failure to thrive." They will turn off, refuse to eat, and become high risks for all sorts of problems, even death. Emotional needs are as important to life support as physical needs.

As human beings move through life, they learn about being careful with emotional investments. They get burned. Certain people reject offers of trust, and it hurts. As a result, people learn to go slowly and offer themselves to deep relationships only with others who have earned trust. By the time most people allow themselves to fall in love and marry, they are very careful indeed. Some people have learned so well about pain and violation of trust that they are unable to invest themselves deeply in any adult relationship. Instead they skim about looking for satisfaction from superficial forms of contact. The need is there within their psyches, but they are unable to fulfill that need.

Almost everyone invests deeply in a variety of relationships throughout life—relationships with family members, friends, spouse, and children. They learn to love and trust these people, knowing they will always be there. If, for whatever reason, someone decides to end one of these close relationships, he or she can go to the person, at least partially withdraw the deposit, and walk away, not unhurt, but still in some control.

When death or divorce ends a relationship prematurely (and prematurity has nothing to do with years but with the unwritten need of each person's psyche), then often what is experienced is the crash of one's emotional stock market. The borders change in one's definition of the parameters of life.

> "I had not planned for my husband to die this year. We were so looking forward to our retirement years."

> "I had to go home from the hospital without a baby, home to the nursery we had just decorated."

> "I never thought my wife could stop loving me. She hasn't found someone else; she just doesn't love me anymore. How can that be?"

Grief is the emotional, physical, and spiritual response to the loss or anticipated loss of someone or something in whom or which one has been invested. Grief is part of the human condition, a part of love. The more one loves, the more acute the pain will be at the separation from the beloved.

THE DYNAMICS OF GRIEF

In the last twenty years, much research has been done on the ways people grieve. Dr. Elizabeth Kubler-Ross was the pioneer. In her work with dying patients, she observed that the journey toward death had certain emotional mileposts and that acknowledging the journey could facilitate a person's way through it. After Kubler-Ross' studies, other people built on her research, developing the school of thought called *thanatology*. This word comes from the Greek *thanatos,* meaning "death". Thanatologists study the nature not so much of death itself (with the exception of some dedicated philosophers) but of the human reaction to death.

Grief counselors refer to the process through which a person must proceed during grieving as *grief work*. Certain tasks must be accomplished in order to withdraw emotional investment from the past, become whole again, and prepare to reinvest in new relationships and realities. Each person accomplishes these tasks in his or her unique way, but most people experience certain typical emotional and physical symptoms. The onset and duration of these symptoms varies greatly and they are often confusing and frightening for the grieving person. As caregiver, your task is to listen to, abide with, and assure the grieving person that these experiences are normal and with time will abate. The pain of their grieving is a sign of their emotional health and a sign of the depth of their loving investment.

However, there is one exception to this. In some cases, you will encounter people who seem to be grieving with extra intensity and cannot move away from the anguish of new separation. In these cases, you as minister must be on the lookout for hidden emotions such as guilt. If the person had a less-than-perfect relationship with the deceased, his guilt may be interfering with the ability to grieve in healthy ways. You will have to assess this guilt. Is it real or imagined? Does the mourner have sound reasons for the feeling or is he or she merely giving in to the "if only's" and "what if's" of normal separation? For example, in the death of a spouse, what may happen to the surviving spouse is that he or she may feel some guilt because the marriage and their relationship wasn't as good as the survivor thought it could have been. Now that the spouse has died, the remaining partner regrets things left undone or unsaid.

If like so many who lose a loved one, the person is only wishing away normal relational fights and thoughtlessness, then when you have heard the story, you can be reassuring. On the other hand, if you judge that there is some serious, underlying, emotional impairment, then while your supportive presence may assist the person to deal with this problem, you will want to help the mourner find a professional person who can be a guide to wholeness again.

One widow I (D.R.W.) visited raved about her husband, the wonderful husband he had been, their happiness while bringing up their children and growing old together, and her pain as he fought cancer for many months. He died just weeks after their children had held a wonderful anniversary party for them. But under all this, I sensed something tenuous, some fear that was preventing her from really allowing these happy memories to heal her.

Glancing about the room, I noticed the heavy oak door, richly carved and very beautiful, that stood open and led out to the front porch.

"Margaret," I said, "Everyone who saw the two of you together knows that you and Jim had one of those really inspirational marriages. It was as rich and special as that lovely door. But the thing that makes that door special is its carving, its depths and heights and swirls. A wonderful marriage is like that. No two intelligent people could live together for over forty years and agree about everything. That kind of marriage is a lie because it means that one person is doing all the thinking and decision making and the other is going along, maybe because he or she is afraid or has a poor self-image. Really good marriages allow room for disagreement and fights, but the fiber is strong; working through things carves a beautiful pattern of highs and lows for all the world to see. When people saw you and Jim together, they knew that you were two people who loved one another enough to relate to each other with honesty and to carve a pattern for your life that was real and wonderful." The woman looked at me with tears in her eyes. "Thank you," she said. "I needed to hear that." Weeks later, she made a special call to my office to tell me that my little analogy had kept her stable at a time when she was having very mixed-up feelings about her marriage. She had shared what I said with her children, and they, too, were helped to see that the patterns of struggle, the interplay of weakness and strength, of good times and bad, were all an essential part of their family's relationship.

Most grieving people don't verbalize their ambivalent feelings, either their love for the person who died or their sadness over things left unsaid or unsettled. Many, many people have ambivalent feelings, sometimes at a subconscious or undefined level, which simply makes them uncomfortable (especially if visitors remark that their relationship with the deceased had obviously been one of deep love and trust).

Besides the grief that occurs after death, there is another kind of grief people experience. It is called *preparatory grief.* Preparatory grief comes before the death. It can be experienced both by the dying person and by those close to the patient and has much the same dynamics as grief after death. For a long time, the prevailing societal attitude in North America was to prevent the dying person and those close to him or her from experiencing preparatory grief. Medical professionals kept stern codes of secrecy. The word "death" was avoided. Dying patients (labeled "terminal") were put into private rooms so as not to disturb other patients and staff. When the person did have the temerity to die, cover-up phrases were invented to pretend that "it" had not happened.

Preparatory grief must be allowed to happen. For the dying person, there will be no other chance to mourn for all that will be lost. For the loved ones, this period before the actual loss allows them time to begin to accept the reality of what will happen and to prepare for the future. For all concerned, this is a time to "mend fences," to say things that need saying and to realize deep healing in wounded relationships.

One place where this healing is especially evident is within the huge and growing community of people affected by Auto-Immune Deficiency Syndrome (AIDS). Many of the people with this horrible disease have become infected directly because of lifestyles that have alienated them from their families. As they become more and more ill, their families begin to draw near, to make overtures at reconciliation. It is natural, when death approaches, to realize that the love between families is more important than external factors. With little time left, people find new ways to say "I love you." These moments can be times of deep joy, but they can only happen if the impending death is recognized and the chance taken to work for reconciliation.

PHASES OF GRIEF

Our first inclination was to entitle this section *Stages of Grief*, but we felt uncomfortable with the word "stages." For many people, that word indicates predictable progression, normal patterns. One thing we know is that each person charts his or her own course on the grief journey, and the caregiver who places expectations on a grieving person is only hindering that journey. Therefore, it is important to assure the mourner that it is normal to experience various physical and emotional symptoms, that there is no set order to the grieving process, and there is a very generous time span. Remember also that every feeling and response associated with grief can happen either *before* an anticipated loss (called preparatory grief) or *after* the loss occurs.

Occasionally, you may encounter a mourner who is stuck. For example, Mr. Wilkins was brought to me (D.R.W.) by his

children because three months after his wife's death. He was
still detached from reality, not sleeping, hardly eating, and
unable to return to work because he could not "hook into" and
concentrate on any task. This type of person needs professional
help to move on with the tasks of grieving.

Use your common sense to determine if an appropriate time
span has more than elapsed. If you err, do so on the side of
allowing the mourner to move more slowly than society expects.
The tasks of grieving allow the person to realize the loss of a
personal investment, accept that loss, heal, and prepare to
reinvest in a life that has new parameters. This must include time
to begin to understand just what that newly defined life means.
What are the new parameters? How can I fit my needs and
expectations into this new life? To recover from the loss of a
spouse, whether through death or divorce, will likely take three
to five years. That may be the time necessary before a person
feels ready to enter into another committed relationship. So
give time to the mourner; your acknowledgment of this need
may be freeing to the person.

Most mourners progress through three phases of grieving:
the acute phase, the transition, and finally, the time of acceptance. When grieving is acute, the pain of loss is just too

---

● *ACUTE*
  numbness, denial

● *TRANSITION*
  anger, bargaining

● *ACCEPTANCE*
  depression
  peace, inner harmony
  wholeness

Table 4.1: Grief mileposts and their characteristics

tremendous to acknowledge, and the mourner may alternate between numbness and denial. The next phase can be called the transition. Gradually, the pain sifts to the surface and the mourner tries to sidestep reality with such ploys as bargaining and anger. The responses in this phase are often the most frightening to those wishing to help ease the pain of the grieving person, but they are necessary responses for someone making the transition from old emotional investments to new ones. Finally reality, which cannot be denied, must be faced and the grieving person is thrown into a pit of despair. It is not a bottomless pit; with support, the mourner will gradually come to a place of acceptance.

Numbness

Early one Sunday morning, I (D.R.W.) was sitting with a woman in the Intensive Care waiting room when the doctor, a young woman, entered and sat down. "I'm sorry, Mrs. Brown," the doctor said. "We've lost your husband." The new widow, exhausted from several days of hospital vigilance, said, "Lost him! Where have you put him?" The doctor straightened herself up and decided to attack this subject head on. "He has passed away," she said. "But where has he passed to?" asked Mrs. Brown. I turned the woman's face toward me, established eye contact, and said, "Mrs. Brown, your husband, Joe, has died. He is dead." I tried to put all my compassion into my voice, but I told her the truth. Realization dawned on her face, and she allowed me to hold her as she cried. After her tears had flowed and she had drunk a cup of tea, she felt ready to enter the room where her husband's body lay to say her last words to him.

This may seem like an extreme case, but as caregiver you need to be aware that grieving persons often miss out on subtlety. Their minds are dulled by their pain. They need clear truth, nothing hard to sort out. They are, after all, sorting out the most painful mystery of life, and denials and euphemisms only add complexity to their task.

For many people, the first phase of grieving is numbness. People have described it as feeling as if they were watching life on a TV screen. "Once in a while, some of the pain of the characters breaks through to me. But they are only characters, and while I am watching the life around me, I am not part of it."

In reality, the person has not accepted the world in which a beloved spouse or child or friend will never live again. Yet the parameters with which the person has defined life are changed. The person needs time for the psyche to adjust to the new parameters.

Mourners may appear glassy-eyed, distracted, forgetful, disoriented. A person may become frightened and say, "I think I am losing my mind." Most mourners do not need medication; drugs will only make the world more fuzzy and as a result, drugged people will not notice being disoriented. The caregiver's job at this point is to be reassuring and explain that they need time to get used to reality. Assure the mourner that this disorientation will pass. Tell the person that you (or someone they can trust) will be there to help do what needs to be done, and that in a few days, his or her mind will be clear again. (Keep in mind that even when the mind clears, deep grief will still remain, and the mourner will need much support.)

Sometimes people who are numb will walk through the days, putting one foot in front of the other, doing all the necessary chores, not seeming particularly disoriented, but not responding in a feeling way to the world. Let them be. Stand by to hold them when their feelings do break through. And be prepared that, when this happens, they may go through the fuzzy, disoriented time after most family members have moved on. This can make a family feel out of sync, and you may need to explain what has happened.

Denial

Mrs. Lowe had driven her father to the hospital late Tuesday evening. He did not want to go, and she had to trick him by telling him she was taking him for a ride to the store. He entered the emergency room protesting loudly and only agreed to be admitted to the hospital after being told that he was having a heart attack. As he was wheeled to the cardiac care unit, he shouted at his daughter, "I told you I didn't need to come; now look what's happened!"

For the next three days, Mrs. Lowe waited beside her phone, hoping that her father would ask to see her. She was afraid to go to the hospital in case he was still angry with her. On the fourth morning, her sister called. Their father had died one hour earlier.

That day, Mrs. Lowe sat on her bed. She did not get dressed, would not speak with her family, and refused to eat. Toward evening, she dressed, took the car, and drove away. Her worried husband followed her. She drove to the same emergency door where she had delivered her father, ran into the waiting room, and began telling everyone in sight that the hospital was hiding her father, had stolen him away from her, and now was conspiring to persuade her family that he was dead. Sympathetic emergency room personnel gently restrained Mrs. Lowe and sedated her so that her husband could take her home.

The next morning, she was at the hospital again, this time at the admitting desk, threatening to call the police if they did not open their records to her. This time she was seen by a psychiatrist, who understood her pain allowed her to explore her own agony. Then, on milder sedation than the previous day, she was taken home. In the morning, Mrs. Lowe awoke saying, "My daddy is dead." It was a flat, emotionless statement, but it was for her the beginning of the grief journey.

Many people begin grieving by denying. It seems nearly impossible to deny reality, but about half of those who grieve do just that. Denial is actually more common *before* death, when a patient and family are told that an illness will gravely shorten life expectancy. Many caring professionals are strong deniers themselves and thus refuse to be honest with ill people and their families, using the excuse that they do not want to take away hope. In truth, medical professionals usually can give a definitive prognosis to the patient. Other caregivers can work in concert with the medical staff to provide psycho-spiritual support.

>Andrew and Felicia had been married for sixty years. For the last three years, Andrew had been growing more and more frail. Felicia could see him deteriorating, and she knew that she would have to accept his death.
>
>Then, Felicia suddenly took ill and went to the hospital with cardiac failure. She stayed in the hospital for the next three weeks, and Andrew sat at home, waiting for her to return. The doctor had issued strict orders that Andrew was not to be told the severity of Felicia's condition because "He couldn't take it." Felicia did not come home. She died, and then Andrew had to deal with his own pain. He did not die. He would not have died had he been told weeks earlier that Felicia's condition was so serious. He would, however, have been able to begin to explore his own fears and to visit his wife with the knowledge that he might not see her again. Would he have spoken to her differently? Who can know? The important thing is that he would have been speaking to himself differently and preparing himself for Felicia's death, which would not have been such a shock.
>
>Andrew felt betrayed by the doctors and his own family. Just because people are old or sick no one is excused from treating them honestly and ethically. It took some time before Andrew could trust again.

On the other hand, many ill people do not accept the honest prognosis given them by their doctors. It is hard for people to accept that in three or six or twelve months, the world will still be carrying on but they will not be a part of it. It is difficult to let go of incomplete dreams and relationships and move on. It is hard to imagine existence somewhere else, in another dimension—what Christians call heaven—to imagine there is life apart from the concrete, familiar world. For those without belief in an afterlife, the thought that life will be "snuffed out," can be frightening.

For the person who has just experienced a shocking loss denial can actually be a useful defense mechanism. Denial allows the person's psyche more time to adjust to the new reality of life. It provides an instinctive cushion so that the psyche will not be so deeply bruised when reality must be accepted. As a caregiver, you can say something like, "I know that all of this is very hard to accept right now and that is certainly all right. You have time. When you want to talk about it, just let me know. I want you to know that I care about you, and will be here when you want me to be."

Denial becomes dangerous and must be addressed when sick people refuse necessary medical treatment because they will not accept the doctor's diagnosis. This often happens when parents find out that their child has a grave illness. They might run from doctor to doctor, even from country to country, looking for someone who will reassure them that their original doctor was wrong, hoping that the pain of accepting this condition can be avoided. Sometimes they encounter charlatans, who offer miracle cures, usually at great expense. All of this prevents patients from receiving medical care that may prolong life or relieve pain. Even sadder is that it wastes precious time when patients and their loved ones could together deal with reality and honestly prepare for the future.

In time, most people will move through denial and begin to accept reality. The time needed for this transition is usually not long. The transition is complicated, however, by the ambivalence that many patients feel: "I might die, and I know I have to accept that possibility, but on the other hand, I need to muster all my energy to try to beat this disease." Is the AIDS patient who refuses to accept the finality of the prognosis and says, "I'll be the first one to beat it," a person of special courage or simply a patient in deep denial? This is a tricky problem to which there are no easy answers. Caregivers must try to encourage hope while sensitively exploring faith possibilities and the "what if's" of dying.

Moving Through Denial

After death one helpful medium for facilitating the move from denial to acceptance is the funeral or memorial service. Neither the spoken words nor the symbols used should convey euphemisms, such as, "She is not dead; she is just asleep." Instead, they should address the loneliness and pain of the mourners. Viewing the body (if that is acceptable in the faith community) helps mourners to accept death as real. Also helpful is the custom of lowering the casket into the grave before people leave the cemetery. Obviously these are times when mourners need special compassion and support, and the caregivers present should be sensitive to their agony. (More about funeral services in chapter fourteen.)

When caring for denying mourners, ask yourself whether they are just allowing their psyches a little time to accept reality or whether precious time for living or seeking treatment is being wasted. If the latter is the case, find out if other people are feeding the denial. If you think you can address the issue, invite the persons involved to move on into acceptance. You might say something like, "Joe, I wish I could say something else to you, but I need to be honest. In the end the choice is yours, but I hope you will consider carefully what I think.

"You have been to three doctors already. Each of them has performed tests, and each of them has told you about the same thing. Their methods differ, but they all say that you have a very serious form of cancer, which they can't cure. They also say that your life can be longer and a lot more comfortable if you agree to certain treatments. Now, I am not certain that it matters if you go with the treatment recommended by the radiologist or the surgeons, but I think you are wasting precious time running to more doctors. Isn't it time, now, to deal with reality and get the treatments you need?" Statements like these still leave control in the hands of the mourner, but you are helping in a discernment process.

If you are helping someone who is grieving for another person's death, you can help them move into acceptance by suggesting some changes in behavior that acknowledge the truth of the situation—perhaps sorting and disposing of the person's belongings, or choosing new social activities. Encourage the mourner to use words that speak directly to the loss, saying "died" or "suicide" instead of "passed on" or "accident."

If you still are unsuccessful in helping the person move out of denial, it is now time to seek help from a professional grief counselor, this could be a social worker, psychologist, or minister—anyone who has special grief support training. Remember that these people will not be able to give you magic answers; their skill is in helping people move through grief, not in removing the pain.

Anger

A common emotion experienced by grieving persons is anger. Anger is halfway between denial and acceptance. Those who deny do not recognize themselves as angry because they have not allowed the painful situation to exist in their mind. (This is not a conscious decision.) If encouraged to move on into acceptance, a person in denial will sometimes burst into great anger, and this anger will often be aimed at the person encouraging acceptance. Through anger the grieving person is admitting that something unpleasant must be accepted, but is not yet ready to give in to reality. (This was the case with Mrs. Lowe's father (p. 42), who shouted at her in the hospital emergency room.)

Grief is always a human response to a situation over which no personal control is experienced. The mourner cannot bring back the person who has died. Usually the mourner did not decide that someone would die. The dying person cannot stop the invasion of cancer, nor can anyone can force his or her heart to continue to beat. Often lack of control causes frustration followed by anger.

From birth people struggle to establish control over their physical, emotional, and professional functions. Sometimes there is a not-so-subtle struggle by young adults when breaking away from parental control. People value independence. When an uninvited force takes over and changes someone's life in a way he or she did not choose, that person can become angry.

We believe that anger is the one universal emotion felt by all mourners. Jesus felt it when he hung on the cross. In both Matthew and Luke, he screamed out, "My God, why have you forsaken me?" This was not the only thing he said. It was one stage on his journey. We believe that no one escapes from crying out an anguished, "NO!" You may never hear the mourning person's anger, but it is happening.

Moving Through Anger

One problem for some Christians is that they see illness and death as acts of God, and therefore they are embarrassed to show their anger. They feel affronted by this external force, but would experience terrible guilt if they admitted their anger with God.

This is a time for caregivers to help them gently explore their image of God. Is God a punisher or a forgiver, a controlling puppeteer or a loving parent? If possible, help mourners see that God does not cause sickness and death; those bad things are part of the reality of life, and they come to good people and bad people without discrimination. Christians believe that Jesus' mission was the defeat death and the offer of eternal salvation. Encourage mourners to stay with their feelings and to trust that God will support them. Try to help them accept God's love and forgiveness. (If you are from a community that celebrates sacramental reconciliation, encourage mourners to use this sacrament as a means to experience God's love.) Help them to understand that God does not promise an easy life to people of faith but promises support and love for the hard times.

Through all of this, do not tell mourners that their anger is inappropriate. You may need to help them evaluate whether the target of their anger really deserves it. If as caregiver you become the target of their anger, it is vitally important to remember that caregivers often receive anger from others. If you can recognize that the anger has nothing to do with you personally, then you can help the hurting person explore the roots of the angry feelings. But if you accept personal responsibility for another person's anger, you will probably burn out very quickly as a caregiver. It is often helpful to share with mourners how their anger feels to you. Often, this open approach will begin to diffuse the tension. Say, "I know you are hurting, but what you keep saying to me hurts. How can I help you with your anger?"

Angela was eleven years old when her father died. She and her parents were riding in the car when a truck forced them off the highway. She could see that her father was gravely injured, but when the ambulances came, they took him to one hospital and Angela and her mother to another. A couple of hours later, the police entered the emergency room where Angela was sitting with her mother and told them that the father was dead. Angela raced at the policeman, pummeling him with her fists and swearing. When he tried to restrain her, she scratched his face.

Rather than put his arms around the child, the police officer chastised her. He told her mother that she was behaving inappropriately and that she must be taken to a psychiatrist. He wrote in his report that Angela was a dysfunctional teen-ager and that he would recommend that she not be allowed to return to school until she received extensive psychiatric care since she "might be dangerous to other children."

This was a child who was yet two years from her teens and had just seen her father killed. Fortunately, a concerned member of her faith community referred the family for grief counseling, and the principal of the her school recognized the police officer's error. Within six months, Angela was playing on the school basketball team, getting normal grades, and returning to a full social life. She never attacked anybody again (although she tells me she did swear at her auntie one day), and, except for a deep sadness, the other children see nothing extraordinary about her. They like her.

The grief counselor helped Angela to understand the feelings she was having and to learn more appropriate ways of expressing anger and other painful feelings. Once the child had vented her pain in the safe environment of the counselor's office, she was able to approach others in non-threatening ways.

This was an extreme case, and most mourners will not actually attack in the animal-like way Angela did. But, given the violence of her experience, it is easy to understand Angela's reaction. Many nurses tell of being the first person to approach a patient or family after a doctor has announced bad news and then left the room. They are sometimes greeted with flying objects or foul language from persons who would normally never be expected to respond violently. These angry people are not responding to life but to death; they see death as an adversary that their normal coping habits cannot defeat.

Anger is a natural and healthy part of grieving, and, with time and understanding, it will usually pass.

Bargaining

Bargaining is another mid-way grief emotion. It is closely related to denial and may occur before mourners can accept the reality long enough to be angry. Or it may occur after mourners realize that their anger cannot change the reality. By bargaining, mourners are, in effect, saying, "Let me think if there is something I can do that will influence some major power figure (God, physicians, parents) to make this painful reality go away." After all, from childhood the power figures have taught, "If you do thus and so, you will get what you want." Some children learn that if they nag enough, their parents and teachers might change their minds. For example, "Just leave me alone and you can go to the party (or have a new bike, or drive the car, etc.)." Perhaps instead of calling this phase of grieving "bargaining," it might just as easily be called persuasion.

In any case, a grieving person sets out to persuade someone to change the situation and sometimes offers a bargain. A child whose parents have recently separated may think that if he behaves well, the parents will reconcile. Or the dead mother may come back to life if the twelve-year-old daughter doesn't allow anyone to speak of her as dead. The patient with pulmonary fibrosis suddenly becomes docile and cooperative, subconsciously saying to his caregivers, "See what a good patient I am? So now you have to make me better." Or the cancer patient experiencing chemotherapy might begin to spend all her free time at church. "God, if you will make me well, I will be a much better Christian, and I will prove that to you by beginning now."

In the First Testament one of the most touching grief bargains was made by Hannah (1 Sam 1:1-23), who sorely wanted a child. Like any normal grieving human being, Hannah tried to strike a bargain with God. She promised God that if she gave birth to a child, she would dedicate that child's life to God. Hannah kept her promise; after she weaned the child, she took him to the temple and left him there to serve the Lord. Did God gift her out of love, or did her bargaining have an effect? Her child, Samuel ("I have asked him of the Lord"), eventually carries God's word to all of Israel. It is not important to know why Hannah conceived. What *is* important is her faith in a loving God. It is possible to imagine that if she had not conceived a child, Hannah's faith in God was firm enough to allow her to move through bargaining to "Thy will be done."

Like Hannah, Jesus himself underwent a conversion. He wanted to change God's plan. This conversion, which took place in Gethsemane, is often referred to as "the agony in the garden." He did not go willingly and docilely to his death, but instead begged, "Please let this cup pass from me." (It is interesting to see how much human behavior and emotion is illustrated in Scripture.)

Like denial, bargaining is natural and not necessarily bad. It gives the grieving person time to gradually get used to the new reality. You do not need to stop the bargaining mourner from praying; if appropriate, share the Gethsemane story and encourage the person to share his or her own anguish. Try to lead gently from the "let-this-cup-pass" moment to "Thy will be done." The family that gathers around the bed of their ninety-three-year-old comatose mother and begs God for a miracle, needs help in understanding that the greatest miracle of all is the promise of resurrection and eternal life. You may also need to help them examine their motives for clinging to someone whose earthly life is over.

Seventeen-year-old Bridget had advanced cancer. Her parents took her out of the hospital and went from one prayer group to another, demanding that God heal her completely. When she experienced a three-month improvement, they held a celebratory service at the church and gave God glory for her "healing." But when she relapsed, they were absolutely dejected. Their faith had been in an "aspirin God" who made things better (ten prayers to be taken as needed). They had no faith context within which to place their daughter's real situation.

About that time, a hospice representative persuaded her parents to admit Bridget to the hospice unit. She was there for several weeks and finally was able to say to her parents, "Please let me go. I need to be somewhere else." With peaceful tears, they held Bridget in their arms until her heart stopped. They certainly did not want to let her go, but they had come to the point in their grieving where they could allow her that freedom and could bear the thought of going on with their own lives after her death.

Bargaining or persuading usually happens because people do not like change; they are afraid to look for alternatives; they do not want to give up the familiar.

Joe, a good friend of mine (D.R.W.), had cancer, a rare and acute strain for which any treatment would only prolong his misery. There was absolutely no hope for a cure. Joe's son, Mario, could not accept that reality, so he began to organize prayer vigils, hoping for a miracle for his father. He thought that more people offering more prayers would be more persuasive to God.

When he called me, I felt caught between two emotions, my need to let him know that he and his family had my support, and my realization that these prayers were preventing his family from dealing openly with each other in the little time they had. I did not want to refuse to pray for my friend, but I definitely did not want to pray as Mario was asking.

So I quietly said, "Mario, I cannot tell God what to do, even though my every wish is that Joe would get better. I would love to join with you in prayer, but I must be honest and tell you that I will pray for God's will. If your father is too sick to get better, I will ask God to take him and heal him in heaven. I don't know why this terrible thing has happened to your family, and it makes me very angry when I even think about it. But I also know that God will take care of Joe, even though we might not understand how that happens. So I will pray that God be in control of this terrible situation. Is that all right?"

To my surprise, Mario started to cry. Somehow my words had helped him to identify his own anger and frustration and to begin to acknowledge the pain of accepting his father's inevitable death. After that day, I decided that telling the truth about my own ambivalence and anxiety did not confuse grieving people but actually helped them. I also realized that it is normal to not know what to pray in these times.

The important thing is really not what people pray but *that* they pray, that they open the lines of communication and relationship with God, even if the communication is about normal human confusion or anger. Try to help the mourner open those communication lines to heaven even briefly. Just as many marriages break down because of external factors that have nothing to do with marriage, so many relationships with God break down because of factors that have nothing to do with God. The breakdown of relationship with God is one of the saddest things a minister can witness.

Depression

One day the grieving person finally realizes none of the familiar coping strategies will work. Crying out in anger did not make the facts ago away. Neither God nor the physicians responded to persuasion or bargaining by giving a miracle cure. At this point, reality sets in.

Many mourners have told us that suddenly a sense of helplessness and hopelessness overcomes them. They were not able to fight off this specter with any of the the coping skills they had learned in life. "It" gets the best of them. There is nothing more they can do and there is no more meaning to life.

The grieving person sinks into a deep pit. For example, one person will not want to get out of bed; a hospital patient may refuse medication, saying, "There's no use, anyway." The person beginning to accept the end of a marriage may not bother to clean the house or may neglect personal habits. Work routines and recreational friends might be neglected. The once committed churchgoer may disappear from community worship services.

Family and friends often become upset at this normal behavior, especially because it often occurs two to three months after the loss. People are less surprised at depression in the first weeks, but they still regard it as a backward step in the grieving process. Far from taking a backward step, this person is finally facing an unpleasant reality, and it is completely appropriate to respond with depression.

At this stage, the caregiver's task is to journey with the grieving person, acknowledging that it is reasonable to feel low and that you, too, get depressed when you think about the loss. Listen to the person's pain, hold the person as the agony grows too strong to bear alone. Christians can reflect on Jesus' agony in the garden. When Jesus knew his fate he only asked his friends to stay awhile with him, as he prayed and wept. He did not ask them to cheer him up or change what was about to happen. When his friends failed him, he asked Peter, "Are you asleep? Had you not the strength to stay awake one hour?" (Mk 14:37). Many hearts have been moved by this story and Jesus' poignant question.

You do not need to give answers to grieving persons or rescue them or cheer them up. On the other hand, you do need to abide with them, support them, and let them know that, whatever happens, you are there for them. Usually the depression will lighten because the human spirit is buoyant and seeks life.

Acceptance

One dying patient said to me (D.R.W.), "I do not need to live, but I do need to understand my death." The wisdom in this statement is profound. We have found it to be true for many, perhaps most, other dying people.

Everyone expects to live. Everyone expects to grow old and watch the younger generation grow up. Everyone plans on becoming wise and mellow before death. Even if someone *is* old and wise, he or she may not be mellow enough to accept death or the possibility of a child or someone beloved dying. Everyone expects to live forever. Since these expectations must inevitably change and the world must always be redefined, there is a need to understand and to find some meaning in the midst of this change called death. When the new meaning is found, a peace will also be found.

Each person finds meaning in a different place, for it is unique. Some people find meaning within their value system and faith. Others look to nature. There are many areas to explore, and the person for whom you are caring may wander about for a while looking for answers. Most emotionally healthy people, after some searching, will find a system into which they can place their reality. When they have found meaning, they may not like the situation any better, but they can accept it.

Remember Bridget, the teen-ager in the hospice unit? At first, she thought her illness had been visited upon her and her family as punishment for some sin, and this thought was achingly painful for her. She could not accept it, so she denied her needs for physical care. But she figured out that God was as sad as she was that young people get sick and that their lives on earth get cut short by diseases and accidents. After she pictured God weeping with her and her parents, she was able to accept her illness as one of those bad things that exist in this world and that attack good and bad people alike. Then she put herself into God's hands. It was not easy to relinquish control over her future, but once she understood, she could do it.

Each person comes to a unique place of resolution. It may be a different place than the one to which you were leading them, but it is not your journey. Your role is to acknowledge the rightness of what works for the person in pain. That is what is meant by "journeying with."

Chapter Five

Symptoms and Duration of Grief

As stated in chapter four, grief is the emotional, spiritual, and physical response to the loss of someone or something in whom or which one has been strongly invested.

Human beings derive a great deal of their self-image from people around them and from the activities that make up their lifestyles. Ask nearly anyone to tell you about himself or herself and the response most often will be, "I am a teacher," or "I am a welder," or "I am married and have seven children." People define themselves by these realities. Very few people will answer, "I am afraid of the dark and I have an ulcer." The external characteristics of a person's life are shared much more readily. Many people carry this identification to such an extent that they have no valid sense of self, aside from the external factors. That is why people jump off buildings when the stock market crashes and why the retirement years are the ones with the highest incidence of suicide among American males.

Every time there is a transition in life people experience grief. Senior students in high school often develop the symptoms of "senioritis," a kind of lethargy and pervading sadness. Another name for this syndrome is *transition mourning*. Students grieve for their familiar self-identity which is about to end. Seniors make promises about keeping in touch and seeing each other after graduation, even though in their "reality-facing" moments they know this will be impossible. These promises are part of the denial stage of grief. They are confused because while they feel a great sorrow inside, people are telling them that this should be a happy time. Confusion and sorrow are two typical symptoms of grief. In more intense situations, especially when the loss has happened through divorce or death, the symptoms will be stronger and often frightening.

Humans are integrated beings. Nothing happens only to the physical body (or the spirit or the psyche) without affecting the other life systems. Therefore when people lose a deep love, they not only feel sad but they usually also develop physical signs of grief. Often these involve the gastro-intestinal system. Stomach aches, constipation, or diarrhea may develop. When this happens sometimes grieving people become frightened thinking that they are developing the symptoms of the same fatal illness that claimed the loved one. This fear is especially common to people who kept long vigils at their loved one's bedside.

Many people have headaches when they are grieving. These headaches are normal, but they are often compounded by the inability to sleep properly and by unpleasant dreams when they *do* fall asleep. As a result, the grieving person is often tired and lacking in energy for activities other than grieving and re-adjusting. This lack of energy can last for some time and is normal. In fact, the return of energy for survival and life enhancement is one of the strongest signs that the person is withdrawing from the former investment and getting ready to reinvest in new relationships.

THE GRIEF CYCLE

Table 5.1 illustrates the typical energy pattern for a grieving person. The circles represent the total energy one has to get through the day. In the first circle, just after the loss, most of one's energy is taken up with grieving re-adjustment, and little

1.

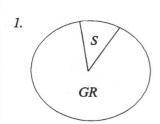

Survival functions, plodding along, unaware

3.

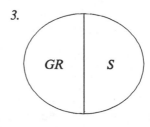

"I feel lighter, its easier." More interest, fulfillment in activites. Makes choices, reaches out to others, finds a hobby.

2.

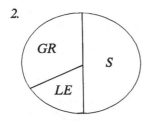

Person able to do what needs to be done in order to exist. "I feel worse now." Person may feel worse because of awareness of what's happening.

4.

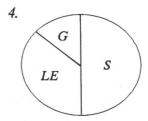

Can't wipe out grieving entirely, or else will lose the memory of person. Grief doesn't restrict except that at anniversaries, etc., grief will reoccur.

Table 5.1. The use of energy while grieving

Above model helpful to people after a loss, e.g., parents after the death of a child deciding when to conceive again. It is based on the amount of energy used for living. GR=grieving re-adjustment, S= survival, LE = life enhancement. *Courtesy of Nancy Reeves, Ph.D.*

energy remains for survival. Survival energy enables a person to get up in the morning, wash, eat—the normal functions of staying alive and living day-to-day. People at this stage may need to be reminded to comb their hair or to eat because all the energy is taken up by the shock of the new reality of life.

After a while, the acute pain dies down a bit, and the portion of survival energy increases. At this stage (illustrated by circle 2 in table 5.1), grievers are coping with the day-to-day necessities in a much more competent manner. Their friends and family may think that the grieving person has fully recovered and may expect that person to begin investing in new relationships. When the person does not feel ready, friends and family become worried. On the other hand, some grieving people feel so much better at this time that they think themselves ready for new relationships.

This is a dangerous time. Widowed or divorced people will rush into new marriages, or couples who have lost a baby will decide to get pregnant again. They know they do not feel happy yet, but they assume that the pain of their loss has changed them in such a way that they will never be completely renewed; so they go looking for new relationships to add some zest to life. In reality, these grievers have only completed about half of their grieving tasks. If they would give themselves more time, they *would* become whole again, rejoice in life, and find new relationships and activities.

Gradually, the amount of energy required for grieving becomes less and survival becomes easier. Then one day, grievers wake up to find the sun shining again. (Move to circle 3 on table 5.1.) A new kind of energy has returned: life enhancement energy (LE). This energy makes people enjoy their friends and activities. It points to a glorious sunrise and finds joy in a child's laughter. This energy makes life worthwhile and defies depression. In healthy people, this makes up about half the energy store.

Eventually the amount of grieving energy expended becomes quite small. (Look at circle 4 on table 5.1.) The tasks of disinvestment are completed, and grievers are ready to find new relationships and activities with vigor and commitment. The pain of the loss never completely leaves, but it becomes small and manageable. Many people say that the remaining, tiny part of pain makes them richer and more fully human. Few people want the memory of their loved one to be completely erased from their mind. But at this point, the memory is no longer terribly painful. It is as if the lost person or dream has a tiny room in the heart of the grieving person. The griever can enter this "room" and remember, or may choose to keep the door closed in order to get on with life.

I (D.R.W.) was working with a family composed of a mother and three children. The mother had been married to the children's father for fifteen years, during which time his addictions had caused her continuous pain. By the time they had been married for ten years, she had completely removed all her emotional investment in the relationship, and the marriage consisted of simple external form so that "the children would have two parents." However, after fifteen years, the wife finally decided that she could not maintain the facade and left, agreeing that the children would spend half their time at each home. At the same time, the mother entered another intimate relationship with a long-time friend, a relationship that both of them hoped would lead to a lifetime commitment.

This entry into a new relationship was healthy for the mother because she had spent plenty of time already grieving for her first marriage, and she was ready to get on with a happy life. The problem was that the children did not realize that their parents' marriage was over until their mother moved out. Because this prevented their normal grieving, they resented their mother's new relationship. They did not understand how she could just "forget" their father so quickly. The mother clung tenaciously to her new friend, who was baffled by the children's violent opposition to his relationship with their mother. During visits to my office, they told me they did not dislike the man; in fact, they didn't know why they reacted so negatively when they saw him with their mother. Their father, who never accepted the end of the marriage, compounded the problem by telling them that he wanted a reconciliation with their mother and that the new man was the reason for the separation. The whole family was confused, especially the mother, who began to wonder if she was indeed doing something wrong. The problem was that she was out of sync with the rest of her family.

I spent some time with the children, explaining the reasons why they and their mother were at different emotional stages in dealing with the "death" of the marriage. I also asked the mother and her new friend to keep a low profile for a while and to give the children time to adjust to the new realities in their lives.

Gradually, as the children accepted the reality of their parents' separation and eventual divorce; as they began to feel more comfortable moving from home to home every few days; and as they learned that their mother making a new life did not mean that she would exclude them, they became less and less

threatened by their mother's new friend. They eventually welcomed him as part of the family, and today they are close friends with him.

Many children in similar situations, however, are simply told they must accept their parents' time schedules. The parents have completed their grief tasks before the separation, but the children have only begun to grieve. It is important to understand the theories of time and energy and the process of disinvestment and reinvestment. These theories can be used when explaining to grieving people the human need for time to adjust to new realities.

GRIEVING THE IMPLICATIONS OF LOSS

In chapter four we said that we do not like to refer to *stages* of grieving because that word often leads people to believe that any deviation is abnormal. In grieving there is seldom an abnormal reaction. On the other hand, it is common for grievers who think they have passed one phase to suddenly experience emotions or physical symptoms they thought they had completed. This re-occurrence of emotions or symptoms occurs because loss has many implications and each of them need to be grieved.

Joan and Benny had been married for eighteen years. One morning on his way to work, Benny fell unconscious in the driveway. Three days later, he was dead. During the time at the hospital, with Benny on artificial life support, Joan went through all the grief stages. At first she called friends, telling them that Benny would be in the hospital for a few days, so she would need help looking after the yard and watching the house. When she began to accept that the few days in the hospital meant that Benny would not be coming home at all, she became angry and shouted at the doctor, the nurses, and God for not healing her husband. Gradually Joan accepted the truth and cooperated with the physicians. She held Benny's hand as the life support system was removed and his heart slowed to a stop.

As her sister led her from the hospital, Joan was exhausted but seemed realistic about her husband's death.

Ten days later, I (D.R.W.) received a frantic call from Joan, who was afraid that she was going crazy. The day before, she had met with her lawyer to go over the financial matters of Benny's estate. Things did not look very good, and Joan was afraid that she would not be able to manage without her husband's help. She woke up the next morning with a huge rage bursting out of her. How could Benny leave her like that? Why didn't the doctors and nurses make him better? What kind of a God would take a fine man in the prime of life?

Joan was worried because she thought she should be finished with anger after all the commotion she had caused at the hospital. Was she moving backward instead of ahead? This was a woman who really wanted to move healthfully through her grief.

I asked Joan why she had been angry in the hospital. She replied, "Because I didn't want it to be happening. I wanted to find someone who would tell me that Benny would not die."

Then I asked her why she was angry that morning. "Because I am worried and mad at Benny (God help him) for not teaching me about our finances and for not leaving things in better order. It's as if he took off and left me holding the pot full of X@#!%."

After Joan verbalized her anger, she understood that she was angry, not at the death of her husband, but at the consequences of his death. Once she realized this, she then felt free to deal with her anger, uninhibited by the fear that she was not grieving properly.

Mourners will move in and out of various emotions, generally moving toward the peaceful end of the scale but with many steps in both directions. One person said that it felt as if he took two steps forward and one step back all along the way. Your task as caregiver is to support and encourage people, assuring them that you will be there for them no matter what.

SHADOW OR ANNIVERSARY GRIEF

Anniversaries of special days are difficult times for grieving people. Wedding anniversaries, birthdays, and religious feastdays can bring a resurgence of grief to people who seem otherwise to be coping well. The weeks before and after an anniversary of a death can bring unexplained depression. This phenomenon is called *shadow* or *anniversary grief.* People often say that they feel lethargic, uninterested in life, depressed, or angry all over again. Suicide rates increase dramatically during the December holidays. Hot lines and emergency rooms prepare for this inevitable influx of business at this time of year, for it is much more difficult to be alone when the whole world seems to be celebrating.

It is important for caregivers to be present to those who mourn during times when grief is likely to come back in unexpected waves of pain. Try to find out important dates so that you can call or drop in on those days. Or ask the mourner to come out with you and do something that will ease the pain. If the person needs to talk, just listen. Talking about the loss may be easier now, since some time has probably passed. Most importantly, be there for the mourner and reassure the person that it is normal to experience shadow grief.

Most experts agree that grief over the loss over a significant relationship usually takes about *four years.* We highlight this time period because many (perhaps most) people find it difficult to accept that it takes such a long time to return to wholeness. This is especially true for people who are lonely after being divorced or widowed. They often want to rush into another intimate relationship; unfortunately, incomplete people have incomplete relationships. As caregiver, you may have to stand aside and allow a person to make this mistake. Frustrating as it is, you cannot prevent adults from doing what they think is best. The challenge for you is to facilitate the person's grieving over the previous relationship while he or she is involved with someone new.

Sometimes, the time spent grieving is significantly shortened if the griever does most of the grief work before the loss occurs. This was the case with the woman whose children did not understand her immediate reinvestment in another relationship (p. 61). If a lover has stood by and watched the beloved gradually die of a long-term illness, the main grief work will already be accomplished. There may actually be a sense of relief when death finally comes. (This does not mean that the person will be happy the next day but duration of grief is shorter than in the case of sudden death. The grief process after an expected death is often more gentle.)

One concern you might have as caregiver is learning to determine whether a person is "stuck" in the grieving process or re-experiencing a phase because of shadow grief. We have stated that people need to be assured and reassured that they are normal and that they need not hurry through grief to please somebody's external timetable. The art of recognizing unhealthy grief comes gradually; it is often part of the counselor's professional instinct, similar to a physician's "sixth sense" for making physical diagnoses. These instincts develop through repeated exposure to similar phenomena.

Generally, if you have reassured the mourner and have explained the grief process, and the person still manifests symptoms that you find frightening or worrisome, it is wise to seek professional advice. If the mourner lingers in long-term self-castigation or depression, or if a couple of years have passed and the person is still in the early, non-coping stage, seek help. If at all possible, try to take the mourner to a counselor who some expertise in grief work; many healthcare and church professionals have never learned how to help persons with "stuck grief" and can intensify the problem. If you cannot make an appropriate referral, hospital departments of social service and chaplains' services can often recommend well-trained professionals.

Many hospitals and civic agencies offer grief support programs at minimal cost. You may do a great service to someone you persuade to enter such programs. In a support group, those who mourn come to understand the grief journey and meet others who are struggling with similar pain. This can be an effective catalyst to healthy grieving. More and more worship communities offer such programs; if your community has not yet done so, you might offer to help develop such a program. (A companion volume to this book designed to train grief caregivers is planned.) Ideally, faith community- based programs allow the grieving person to make the grief journey accompanied and supported by people with similar values.

Most importantly, believe in yourself and your ability to help those who are experiencing this type of intense emotional pain. Once you understand the normal behaviors and emotions of grieving people, your main task (other than praying) lies in reassuring those who mourn that they are normal and that gradually things will improve.

Chapter Six

Person-to-Person Skills

*No one can have greater love than to lay down
his life for his friends (Jn 15:13).*

The Scripture passage above speaks of a vital aspect of
listening. To listen attentively to another person is to lay down
your life for that person. During his time of need, you let go of
your needs, judgments, and solutions. You are present to
another in a life-giving manner, ready to receive his reality. You
become, simply, a loving and open person to the other and set
aside your own agenda and expectations.

To listen in this manner may entail for you a radical change
in attitude and behavior. In Western society, people are accus-
tomed to giving answers, defending, and explaining. Try to put
aside those habits. As you listen, become aware of the other
person as unique, created and loved by God, andbecome aware
of God's desire to lead that person to wholeness and life. Your
task is to help him or her discover personal, inner resources,
and the presence of God. Thus it is important that you, the
listener, have a relationship with God and that you trust the
Spirit of God at work in the other person. This does not mean
that you force your faith experience on the other person. The

task of the caregiver is to enable people to find *their* inner strengths (which for some will lead to an experience of God.)

Pay attention, come to me; listen,
and you will live (Is 55:3)

Communication is essential to all relationships, relationships with God and with people. The healthier the communication, the healthier the relationship. In a scriptural sense, when people communicate they open themselves to new life and they collaborate in bringing forth new life in others.

Instances of listening and communication bringing about change and new life can be found throughout Scripture. Matthew's story of the Canaanite woman is one example of communication (Mt 15:21-28). The woman begs Jesus to make her daughter well. Because she is a Canaanite, a pagan, Jesus informs her that he was only sent to the Jews, not to pagans. She continues to reason with him, and ultimately Jesus cures her daughter. The dialogue with the woman appears to have changed Jesus' response to her. The woman's ability to communicate her needs and her understanding of her relationship with Jesus has brought her to experience a new sense of inclusion. The changes in both the woman and Jesus would not have happened if they had not communicated.

Christians live the reality of God's intense desire to communicate and relate with human beingsandthey believe that because of this desire God became human in Jesus.

He emptied himself, taking the form of a slave,
becoming as human beings are (Phil 2:7).

Just as God gives to you through Jesus, so you can make a gift of yourself to those to whom you are called in ministry. Listening is a gift of yourself to others made possible through your relationship with the God.

Listening skills can be learned, but they are more than mechanical techniques. They are, in fact, the enfleshment of your love, care, and empathy for others. This is why in order to learn and use the skills you need to be aware of your own feelings and understand that your ability to really listen will flow out of who you are as a unique person.

FEELINGS IN SCRIPTURE

Throughout the books of the First Testament, people struggle to understand and act upon their emotions. In the book of Job, Job speaks his anger, desolation, and frustration and he also speaks his faith.

> *Job spoke next. He said: "How much longer are you going to torment me and crush me by your speeches? You have insulted me ten times already: have you no shame at maltreating me? Even if I had gone astray, my error would still be my own affair. But, whereas you take this superior attitude and claim that my disgrace is my own fault, I tell you that God has wronged me and enveloped me in his net. If I protest against such violence, I am not heard, if I appeal against it, judgment is never given. He has built an impassible wall across my path and covered my ways with darkness...I know that I have a living Defender and that he will rise up. (Jb 19:1-8, 25-26.)*

Perhaps one reason that the Psalms are so popular, especially as helps in prayer, is that they clearly present the whole range of human emotions: fear and hope, joy and desolation, triumph and rage. Like country western music, the Psalms are about human emotional experience, often without reference to the historical events which form so much of the First Testament. In that sense they are timeless. Millions of people have identified with the Psalms when they searched the Bible for scriptural texts that make sense of their own experience.

The authors of the Second Testament have a different image of God because of Jesus. Jesus, whom Christians believe is God and fully human, naturally experienced the full range of human emotions including helplessness, desolation, joy, and love.

In many places, the Gospels show Jesus as a person who experienced and expressed feelings. For example, when his friend Lazarus dies, Jesus went to the tomb with Mary and Martha, Lazarus' sisters. When he saw their tears, he felt their sorrow (and his own) and he wept. The Jews said, "'See how much he loved him'" (Jn 11:35).

Jesus expressed anger when he saw that the people were obstinate and unwilling to accept his cure of a man on the Sabbath. "Then he looked angrily round at them, grieved to find them so obstinate" (Mk 3:5).

Jesus knew joy, especially as he experienced God at work in people. When the disciples returned from the places he had sent them to minister, he listened to them as they told of what they had done in his name. "At this time, filled with joy by the Holy Spirit he said, 'I bless you, Father, Lord of Heaven and of earth, for hiding these things from the learned and the clever and revealing them to little children'"(Lk 10:21).

Jesus lived deeply his own reality as a human person. He didn't just pretend to have feelings; he felt because it is human to feel.

FEELINGS AND THE CAREGIVER

Whether faith is based in the First Testament or is centered in the Second, believers today are often taught to deny and repress their feelings. Over the years, society has been influenced by various philosophies and cultural values such as Stoicism and Puritanism which attempt to negate human weakness and emotion. The Western world emphasizes strength and control and "putting up a good front." This mentality encourages people to deny their feelings and then they become unable to name the emotions they are experiencing.

Even when children experience hurt or anger, they are often chided and told to be strong and not be crybabies. People learn to judge their emotions; they learn to judge that anger, resentment, sadness, and other "negative" emotions should not be expressed. How often have you been told, or have you told someone else, "You shouldn't feel that way"?

Feelings are not rationally chosen; they rise up within. Emotions have no morality. They are neither right nor wrong; they simply *are*. All feelings must be accepted and validated. Only then are people able to decide how those feelings will affect their lives. Traditionally, some Christians thought that the best way to deal with "negative" emotions is to "offer them up."

Feelings must be named and acknowledged in order to experience inner freedom and clarity. This acknowledgment enables deeper relationships, both with God and others. Once you name and claim a feeling, you can make choices about your behavior. Unacknowledged and repressed feelings often affect your behavior in a negative way even though you may not know why.

David, a priest for twelve years, was tired. He had been three years in a parish composed of mainly retired people, and he usually celebrated three to five funerals each week. He baptized very few children and celebrated only a handful of weddings. Sometimes, it seemed to him that his ministry was situated right at the end of life.

David had never really felt comfortable about death before coming to St. Vivian's. He had especially enjoyed youth ministry and preparing engaged couples for marriage. But he had been sent to this older parish, and nobody had asked him about his feelings.

Gradually through the years, David's resentment built up. It began to affect many areas of his ministry. He refused invitations to attend parish functions because he thought that there would be no "life" there, only old people. He often did not return telephone messages, and he shut himself inside the rectory much of the time. When he was called upon to celebrate a funeral, he would do so with the most cursory preparation and without personal contact with the family.

Finally one day, Mark and Janet, a couple who led several parish groups, came to visit him. They did not call and ask for an appointment; they just turned up and said, "It is important that we see Father David right now." So he allowed them into his study.

Mark and Janet came right to the point. "Father, we are worried about you. When you first came to St. Vivian's, we knew that you were not happy. We could tell because you were not sociable and hardly smiled at anyone. We thought that you were lonely for your last parish. Several of us spoke about the problem, and we all decided to give you time and to be friendly and invite you to get to know us so you would feel more like one of the family.

"But you've had a long time, Father, and you seem even more unhappy.

"To be honest, St. Vivian's needs a priest who will get involved, who will care about us. We don't know what your problem is, but we came to see if we can help. You should know that several people are thinking of petitioning the bishop for your removal because the parish is dying under your leadership.

"Please, Father David, let us understand what is making you so unhappy, and let us try to help."

David's attention was centered on these good people who had cared enough about him to try to help him even though he had never bothered to care about them. What had blinded him to their goodness and to the goodness of so many others in the parish? He realized then that he had been nursing his own prejudices and his resentment about being sent to St. Vivian's parish. He had been refusing to respond to the reality around him because of feelings within himself. Once he realized what he had done and admitted that to Mark and Janet, they were together able to begin picking up the pieces of his negative ministry and helping the people of St. Vivian's find their sense of family again.

Thus, in order to be a good caregiver and to help others express their feelings, try to name what you yourself are feeling. Sometimes you will not be aware of having feelings, but your body will help you. Feelings are registered in the body, often in the arms, shoulders, neck, head, or stomach. One person's unexpressed anger results in a headache, another person develops an ulcer.

If you are unaccustomed to paying attention to your feelings, start with being aware of and listening to your body. What bodily sensation are you feeling? Pinpoint the area of your body, then ask yourself, "What emotion am I feeling? Is my heartbeat rapid or slow? Is there tension or pain in any area of my body? Is that tension connected to any emotions or experiences I've had today?" Try to name the feeling, choosing a word that describes most exactly what you are feeling. Then describe the feeling in writing and allow yourself to really experience the fullness of the feeling without judging it.

This process can help you to accept your reality, to receive what is in your life at the moment. After going through and entering your inner reality, you become truly able to say "Yes" to the way God made you. Once you have surrendered to your authentic self, (feelings and all) and accepted yourself humbly, you will become peaceful and relaxed. You cannot change and grow unless you are able to accept what *is*.

THE PASTORAL VISIT

Although you may have fears about your initial visit to a stranger, remember that those who mourn feel worse pain when they find that nobody cares enough to visit them when they are hurting. What you say is not nearly as important as your presence.

But you want to be more than just a presence; you want to make the love of God real to the person you visit. Before the visit, the most important thing you can do is pray. Ask God to help you and enable you to truly listen. Try also to do some advance investigation about the people and their living situation. Through this investigation you may become aware of some issues the grievers might need to discuss. You will be more focused and secure, able to help the hurting people talk about sensitive areas rather than chatter superficially.

Introductions

Special sensitivity is needed when visiting someone in the hospital. Often people come into and leave a patient's room without saying who they are or why they are there. A person's hospital room is home for the moment. For many, it is the last home on this earth. That is why when you enter, you should knock, introduce yourself, and ask permission to visit. Your actions acknowledge that the sick person is still in control.

Similarly, when you visit a home, do not assume you are welcome. Always introduce yourself, tell why you have come, and ask permission to stay. Your exchange might go something like this:

"Hello, Mr. Wilson. I am Rita Smith from Central Methodist Church. We heard you have been sick, and Pastor Tom asked me to come over and bring you the love and prayers of our church family. May I spend a few minutes here with you?"

This introduction validates you as a representative of someone familiar and as a person of faith. It also defines the time limit of your visit, which is important because sick or grieving people do not have much energy for social conversation.

If you visit somebody who already knows you, it is important to define the role you are taking for this visit. You might say, "Mary, I heard about your daughter's accident. I'm sorry. If you would like to talk, I am here to listen." Your message to the person is that you are available: you are there to help. But allow the person to respond freely. If the person decides not to talk about a specific issue, accept both the decision and the person just they are.

Establishing a Climate for Listening

With your voice and body language, you establish the environment of the room. You will seldom be on your "own turf," so you must try to develop a climate of trust wherever you are. In the hospital, do not hesitate to pull the curtain around the bed of the patient you are visiting. This action signals to everyone, "I am here for something important." If the curtain is pulled, and if the person chooses to talk about intimate concerns, you are less likely to be interrupted by hospital personnel coming in and out. Sensitive people will only bother you for matters that cannot wait.

Messages are communicated by posture and position relative to another person. If you appear relaxed, the person will get the

impression that you are open and receptive. If you stand up, you exert a feeling of superiority and control over someone confined to a bed or chair. Crossed arms and legs communicate that you are closed in and distant. On the other hand, an open posture, with your arms folded in your lap and your body leaning slightly forward says that you are available and open to what the person has to say. Your posture can tell a person, "I want to be here with you, for whatever you need."

Eye contact can be either reassuring or frightening. You will learn to gauge the reaction of the other person. Always try to establish eye contact, but if the person evades your efforts, be tactful. Many of the most intimate conversations happen when two people both face the same direction, as when walking or riding in a car together. This position may seem more safe for people who are insecure of their acceptance. Especially with young people, it is often better not to demand too much eye contact until the relationship is established.

On the other hand, when a person responds positively to your initial eye contact, try to maintain this demeanor. Looking away on your part can signal, "I am getting bored with this conversation." If you have difficulty looking at the other person you, this may be a signal that you yourself may not be comfortable with the topic or with the intimacy of the situation. Try to tune in to what is going on inside you so you can deal with your perceptions honestly.

Try to be relaxed, natural, and in touch with yourself as you choose ways to communicate that you are present with the other person. These skills will begin to flow naturally from your love and concern for the person. You need to find your own ways— through physical posture and behavior—to show your care. If your response rises from genuine compassion and a sense of who you are yourself your pastoral presence will flow from your concern.

What Do I Say?

By now, you have introduced yourself and established, through your relaxed and open posture, a comfortable environment. Your next step is to use a few skills to guide the conversation without assuming control. Open questions are often helpful; they do not demand a specific answer, but instead open doors to sharing and indicate your willingness to listen. You might say, "Would you like to talk about that?" or "Is that something that worries you?"

People are not usually encouraged to share their feelings, and the people you visit may not know what they feel about the situation. If the person brings up sensitive material but does not explore it fully, you could respond with one of the following:

"I'm sensing that it's difficult for you to express what you are really feeling. Am I right?"
"What is happening inside you right now? Can you help me to understand what you are feeling?"
"How do you feel about that?"
"What's that like for you?"

If the person seems not to want to burden you with the pain, assure them, "I am here to listen."

Rejection of Your Visit

People who are very ill, or grieving, or both, are subject to an onrush of painful emotions. They struggle to sort out their own reality and to find ways to continue living with it. Your sudden appearance may just be too heavy a burden that day (especially if they sense that you want to speak of personal issues). Or they may feel too unwell for any more stimulation, no matter how gentle and loving.

Another person, someone unexpected such as the cleaning lady or the man who comes to fix the blinds, or a visiting neighbor, may be meeting the needs of this hurting person. This can be hard to take when the person you plan to help with all your professional expertise tells you, "Thank you, but no thanks. I am already talking with my grocer about these things. He has really helped me, and I am satisfied. I would like to talk about ordinary, everyday things with you."

It is essential to maintain a sense of balance (and humor!) about your importance, and recognize that God has gifted many people besides you. If the grieving person is coping without your help, or even if the person is not coping very well but does not want your help, you should back away gently, in a caring and respectful manner.

Read the example story on page 98. Ask yourself how you would react if someone spoke to you as Mary spoke to Pastor

Jethro. In this case, the minister acted wisely and helped Mary
sort out her pain.

When I (D.R.W.) was a trainee chaplain working in the
Neo-natal Intensive Care Unit of a large hospital, babies died
every day. Part of my job was to liaise between the medical
people and the parents and to be a support person for both.
The hospital had a policy that the chaplain was to be notified
whenever death was approaching.

One day, I had a call from NICU and, upon arrival to the unit,
I was met by a doctor who told me in an angry voice, "Baby Jones
just died. I am telling you because I'm supposed to, but stay
away from the parents. The last thing they need right now is
someone spouting religion at them." With that, she marched
away.

I wandered into the hallway, wondering what to do. In the
hospital hierarchy, the doctor is in control. I was just a student.
I had to do what the doctor said. Plus, I was hurt, judging that
the doctor had meant that I, personally, could not help the
grieving parents. So I stayed away from the unit so that the
nurses would not think I was hanging around or getting in the
way.

The next morning, as I entered the unit, a nurse called to me
right away, "Joan (the mother) has been asking for you, and we
didn't know how to get you." I went into Joan's room to find
her with the baby's father (both were teen-agers). Both were in
tears. I had been with them when their baby was born a few days
earlier, and I had not gone to them on the day their son died.
They told me they had repeatedly asked for me because they
wanted to plan a funeral for their tiny baby.

I learned some important lessons from this case. The first is
to ask the patient myself if she wants me around. The second is
that I took personally the doctor's angry reaction to so many
babies' deaths. I forgot that "spouting religion" is not what
chaplains do, and I had spent the evening thinking that perhaps
chaplains did not have a place within the hospital structure. In
other words, I allowed one person's angry reaction to death to
send me out of the hospital and away from helping anyone that
evening; I spent all evening fussing and worrying about my own

credibility; I even loitered in the lower floors of the hospital the next morning, thinking that everyone up on the units considered my ministry a waste of time. I recognized the fragility of my own professional identity, but also the fragility of my faith that God called me to this ministry.

I would like to say that I have never repeated that mistake, but it would not be true. Every time a person thanks me but tells me that my ministry and presence are not needed(some do this in kinder ways than others), I once again enter into self-castigation and doubt. But now I don't allow myself to wallow. I know that God has called me, and I know that many people want what I have to offer. I also know that many people turn away from God. I examine my own need to save the world by myself, and finally I laugh at myself and regain my balance.

LISTENING TO NON-VERBAL COMMUNICATION

In any spoken communication, only a small part of the message is understood from the spoken words. Much more is communicated through the speaker's tones of voice and non-verbal behaviors. Unfortunately most people pick up these unspoken clues only subliminally and do not understand or take the time to sort through how they really can impact the communication.

The competent caregiver takes time to really listen to the whole message—both the words and all the possible meanings behind them. It is especially important to search for feelings that the speaker may be expressing only indirectly because it is to feelings that caregivers can most effectively respond.

A nurse may find that a certain patient is expressing discontent with many factors of hospital routine. Rather than assume that this person is just a complainer, the nurse might gently try to find out if there is some other source of stress. Often people who express strong fear of death are actually afraid of concrete things. It helps to ask specific questions.Perhaps physical pain or fear about aging, illness, or death is the real reason for the grumpiness.

I (D.R.W.) recently asked a man who was dying to tell me what he envisioned death would be like. I did not say "life after death" because this man had not expressed a belief in any afterlife. I thought that the actual moment of death might be what was worrying him so I left the question open to his interpretation.

"I think death will be like the desert, dry and empty and ugly, with cold wind and sagebrush blowing around," he answered.

"That's a pretty bleak picture," I said. "Can you tell me why you think it will be that way?"

"Well, my life has been pretty bleak already. I've done a lot of things that nobody likes. I've used drugs and lived on the streets and stolen, and I haven't seen my family for years. Why would I get anything better after I die? No, I think I'll likely spend eternity in a desert."

I now understood that not only did my patient have a concern about an afterlife, but he also had already judged and sentenced himself. Now I could dialogue with him about his perceptions of God and of reconciliation and forgiveness. By the time he died, this man was able to journey peacefully because he believed that he had something to offer to God and that God was interested in him.

Caregivers should always listen for the feelings behind words. There are many ways to do this. Learn to read body language. Does the person look tense or self-protective, even though the spoken message is denying any tension? People who are upset often do not even understand their own feelings and they may not be intentionally hiding anything from you. Your attempts to understand may actually help them to understand their feelings. You can say something like, "Andy, I'm not trying to pry, but you seem to be worrying about something today. Is there something troubling you? I'd like to help, even if all I can do is listen." This type of inquiry allows the person to begin to process inner tension and also decide whether to share with you or not. It shows your respect for the other's privacy as well as your concern and support. If the person still responds that there is no problem, then just say, "Well, I'm glad that I was wrong, but I do want you to know that if you ever need a listening ear, I am available."

NAMING THE FEELINGS

You might find that you are one of those people with well-developed instincts for unspoken feelings. This is difficult to describe, but, if you have this gift, you will understand what we mean. Many people have an uncanny ability to pick up "vibes" from others that may tell them more about the person's inner life than even the person herself knows.

Usually, people fall into one of two groups: sensate or instinctive. Either you notice a great many accurate details about the physical environment, or you hone in on the unspoken interaction in the room. Think about the last time you were in a large gathering. Could you recount now all the colors of the room's decor? Do you know what each person was wearing? Do you know who was wearing glasses? If so, you are in the class of people with strong sensate abilities. You can likely find your way easily even in neighborhoods you don't know well. You may easily remember phone numbers and prices of purchases. These are some of your talents.

Then there are those of us (the authors included!) who still get lost a few blocks from home. We can't describe people after an hour's visit, although we may have come to know the person well. We know that we have to write down date and phone numbers or we will forget them. We can spend hours at a party and not know what anyone was wearing. We might not know the color of paint in our own offices (although the color of paint may have strongly affected our mood while in those rooms).

Instead, we both will have a pretty good idea of all the subtle interactions going on in that party group. This is our talent. We seem to have invisible antennae for picking up feelings. This can be a useful gift for caregivers, but it must be honed and used responsibly. We learned to read our own instinctive messages, process them and check them out, before we act on them. When we do this, we become tremendously effective at helping others to understand their own feelings and motivations. We also always remember to respect the right of the other to tell us we are wrong.

Whether you fall into either the sensate or the instinctive group, you can become a more effective caregiver if you remind yourself to be aware of the feelings behind the words being spoken. Ask yourself, "What might this person be feeling?" Find a feeling word that might describe the emotion and offer a tentative statement along those lines: "You sound lonely" or "You seem to feel hurt." Let the person tell you if you are correct. Obviously, the person always has the final word.

Keep in mind that while you may give a different name to the person's emotion than the one chosen by the mourner, you might still be close. For example, many people are reluctant to name themselves "angry" or "mad" because of the negative connotations society puts on these words. People might feel more comfortable with, for example, "frustrated" or "fed up." If you allow them to use the less-intense labels for their feelings at first, it might be easier for them to really own their feelings. Later on, when the feelings have become more familiar to them, they might be able to apply stronger labels.

The chapter thus far has concentrated mainly on identifying and acknowledging feelings. If you can help hurting people understand their feelings, you will assist them through the grief experience and prevent them from getting stuck in one phase . For some, experiencing feelings may be their key to beginning the grief journey, which they may have avoided until your help. Keep in mind that grief must be experienced, and the sooner the better. Unacknowledged grief will come back to haunt the individual later in life.

Your acceptance of "darker" feelings affirms people as lovable human beings. Everyone needs that assurance, but especially those who mourn. They no longer have confidence in the capabilities they had before their loss. They need to know they are still loved and trusted, in spite of feeling weak and helpless at this time.

As a caregiver, you are privileged to have opportunities to reflect to others the compassion and unconditional love of God. Sometimes this is difficult; certainly, alone, you are not always capable of responding compassionately to those you find unattractive or whose behavior or ideas differ radically from your own. With prayer, however, you can open yourself to God and allow God to flow through you, God's love to permeate you. Only then can you reach out to another in a fully loving and accepting manner. To find out if you are really allowing the other person to tell you their true feelings, discern whether you are responding out of empathy or out of sympathy.

EMPATHY OR SYMPATHY?

People generally approach life experiences with a certain personal mind-set. Usually people who feel called to be caregivers experience an element of "feeling the pain of others" in their call. This feeling can propel the caring individual to share or lift the burden of those who are hurting. For Christians, this urgency incarnates Jesus' words: "If anyone wants to be a follower of mine, let him renounce himself and take up the cross every day and follow me" (Lk 9:23).

There are different attitudes with which you can approach a hurting person. Two of these attitudes are *empathy* and *sympathy*. It is helpful to understand the difference between the two and to discover which one is operative in you.

Both empathy and sympathy may evoke tears. Tears of sympathy flow because you feel sorry for the person in pain. Tears of empathy flow from actually *feeling* a small portion of that pain. In sympathy, you are on the outside looking in; in empathy, you have, as the Native Americans say, "crawled in through the person's feet, up through her belly, felt the pain of her chest, and are looking at the world through her eyes."

Sympathy is not a very productive pastoral stance. In fact, it often makes people feel their burden more heavily because the grieving person can feel responsible for the pain and tears of the sympathetic caregiver. It may also add embarrassment to the grieving person's list of painful feelings. Empathy, on the other hand, allows the person to feel understood, which can often significantly reduce the pain.

If you are wondering whether you are sympathetic or empathetic, ask yourself some questions:

1. Do I think that I might find a solution for this person or make her situation better? If you answer "Yes," you may be feeling sympathy. Empathetic caregivers often are so much "into the space" of the hurting person that they understand the problem may have no immediate solution.

2. Do I feel sorry for this person, or do I feel simply sorry that the person is in so much pain? If you feel sorry *for* the person, you are likely feeling sympathy. If you feel sorry *that* the person is hurting, you are likely feeling empathy.

Empathy is the ability to feel what another is feeling without losing yourself in the other's pain. You really share the other person's experience, but you remain yourself. Empathy implies acceptance and support. If you read the story of Job, you will see that Job's friends have a great deal of sympathy for him, and they try to give him lots of advice about how to change his situation, but they do not empathize. They hold themselves aloof and gloat in their own good fortune.

Empathy journeys with the hurting pain in the same way the psalmist experiences God:

> *Even were I to walk in a ravine as dark as death I should fear no danger, for you are at my side (Psalm 23:4).*

RESPONSES THAT ARE NOT HELPFUL

Most people have both received and given responses that are not helpful. In fact, some responses may have prevented any beneficial communication. Competent caregivers may need to act in ways different from society.

When caregivers find themselves preaching, advising, lecturing, or probing those who mourn, they can be trying to be helpful, but usually they accomplish the opposite. The grief journey can only be undertaken by grieving people and only along their own pathways. You can help a grieving person identify the pathway, but you can neither walk along it before the person nor ask the mourner to walk your pathway. As a grief supporter, you can walk with the one who mourns (a bit behind), and you can allow the person to tell you what it is like. You are companions on the journey, but it remains the mourner's journey.

> Recently, I (J.S.) heard a friend say to a man who had been diagnosed with terminal cancer, "None of us knows when we'll die. I could be dead before you. Cheer up." This type of message was not helpful; it was a denial of the actual condition and a subtle put-down. Not only did it make the sick person feel worse, it also probably created guilt, because no matter what, the person could never take the friend's advice and "cheer up." How much more helpful if the friend had just honestly acknowledged his own fear and anger at the diagnosis and allowed the sick man to share his own feelings?

Though you may think you have the answers to another person's problems and are thus inclined to offer advice, your role is to help him discover and reach his own solutions. You may help by giving information, ideas, or insights such as "Have you ever considered...?" or "Did you ever think of...?" In contrast, at other times you may be called to just sit in the impasse with the person.

In this scientific and technological age, people often try to interpret and figure out every situation. Many of the problems in life that contained an element of mystery for earlier generations have now moved into human control. There are now answers for most questions, solutions to most problems. Therefore, when something comes up that has no predictable solution or reason, people become confused and often panic. Most people today are not comfortable with mystery and will struggle to find a solution in order to regain control.

This is fine when one is struggling to control one's *own* life. Unfortunately, many people extend the struggle to finding answers to the problems of other people. The difficulty is that the answers they find might satisfy *them*, but the answers are not at all suitable for the person who really has the problem.

The task of the caregiver is to continually ask, "Whose problem is this?" If it does not belong to you, do not try to give it your answers. Instead, even if the other person asks you for answers, try to help discern what that person experiences. It is fine to admit, "I don't know the answer to that either. I have struggled with this question, and I can tell you some of the thoughts I have had. But in the end, you might not agree with my thoughts. Some questions seem not to have any pat or easy answers. Maybe that's part of the nature of human life."

What *is* possible is to reassure people of God's loving presence, and tell them that God weeps with them. Later, grievers may find meaning in this sorrowful event. Your love, support, and presence will facilitate this movement toward meaning. Through your care people may in turn experience God's love and support. You might find it helpful to read the story of the death and resurrection of Lazarus (John 11). As was mentioned before, this story illustrates that Jesus, even though divine, felt the pain of his grieving friends and wept with them.

> I (J.S.) was visiting a woman whose husband had been murdered. She was experiencing tremendous loss and pain. As she told me about the death and the impact it had on her and her six-year-old daughter, she also told me how difficult it had been for her to answer people's questions. Many people asked her for details about the murder. They did not ask questions in an effort to comfort or console her, but only to satisfy their curiosity. This was not helpful and only increased her agony.

As a caregiver, you try to be sensitive about probing. Probing for facts (as in the above situation) is not helpful. Probing in order to help people talk and clarify their own experience, on the other hand, *is* a helpful skill. You need an on-the-spot ability to sense whether your probing will serve the wounded person's needs or your own.

If you find yourself preaching, advising, or lecturing, you may be trying to avoid feelings that you perceive as frightening or painful. Or you may be trying to fill silence with words. You can't say anything to make the journey easy; that's like trying to find a clear path through the jungle. All you can do is provide some tools to cut away the leaves and vines. You can make the journey less laborious by saying "I'm sorry" and not offering easy solutions which only tend to belittle the pain.

PORTRAIT OF A HEALING MINISTER

The following are four fundamental attitudes essential for the healing minister. They provide the foundation for your listening and helping skills. They are God-given and God-like qualities and each person has the potential to develop them. These attitudes form a basic portrait of a caregiver.

1. *A genuine love for the other.* This is a non-possessive love, which accepts others just as they are and desires the best for them. If you do not truly love the other in this sense, you will probably not be able to help. When this kind of love is in action, God is at work.

2. *A non-judgmental attitude.* The person to whom you minister may not share your moral standards, values, or behavior. But that is the other person's lived experience, and it is from this reality that the mourner will journey. You are not there to condemn, but to help. Your stance is to want what is good for the other and to assist the person in moving through the pain.

3. *Faith in the other.* With this attitude, a minister believes that hurting people have within themselves all that is needed to solve their problems, all that is needed to discover the steps toward peace and wholeness. Each person has an inner life; the Spirit of God lives within everyone. You can help others dis-

cover their own sources of faith and liberate the life and resources within them.

Faith in the other has a positive effect on growth and change.
Jesus empowered and transformed people. When he met the
woman at the well, he saw beyond her identity as a woman and
as a Samaritan. He revealed God's promise to her as well as his
identity as Messiah. She was them empowered to tell this "good
news" to others.

> *The woman put down her water jar and hurried
> back to the town to tell the people, "Come and
> see a man who has told me everything I have
> done; could this be the Christ?" (Jn 4:28-29).*

4. *Genuineness and honesty.* Living this attitude means to both
be aware of your inner reality (including feelings) and to express
this inner reality honestly and clearly. This means that if you do
not understand the experience or values of the person you are
ministering to, do not pretend that you do. Genuine caregivers
communicate both a deep interest in understanding and an
honesty about the struggle.

Being in the presence of someone who is honest and true,
enables those who mourn to enter their own truth. For Christians, Jesus is the best example of being genuine and honest.
Time after time, he spoke the truth; he did not pretend to be
other than what he was.

> *They were overcome when they saw him, and his
> mother said to him, "My child, why have you
> done this to us? See how worried your father and
> I have been, looking for you." He replied, "Why
> were you looking for me? Did you not know that
> I must be in my Father's house?" (Lk 2:48-49).*

This chapter focused on several different insights and skills
which can improve the effectiveness of your response to
another's pain. But learning to be a caregiver is not like learning
to drive a car. When driving you discipline yourself to push away
internal experiences in order to concentrate on what is happen-

ing around you. As a caregiver, you do just the opposite. The more you learn to pay attention to your internal experiences, the more effectively you will respond to another's pain.

Chapter Seven

Death and the Journey Within

Illness, suffering, and death often lead people to question the meaning and ultimate significance of life. In times of acute crisis, answers which come from sources outside the self are frequently found useless. People then begin to look within for solutions.

As a caregiver, one of your tasks is to help people come to terms with the reality of who they are and what their lives mean. You can help others both define and learn to use their own personal and faith resources. This task is the spiritual (or religious) aspect of pastoral ministry.

Defining the term *spirit* is nearly as difficult as pinning down the wind. But for the purpose of this discussion, we are using the term *spiritual* in this way. *The spirit is the animating life force or principle that is unique to human beings.* It is the ability to transcend oneself and to perceive meaning and direction in life. Even though someone does not profess a religious belief, he or she has spiritual values and resources. Many people also have a religious expression of their spiritual values. They participate in a system of beliefs and a community which follows a particular form of spirituality (understood as relationship with God).

Table 7.1 briefly summarizes many of the spiritual and religious aspects of caring for dying people. The table is divided into three sections: past, present, and future. In actual experience, such definite parameters do not always exist; however, these divisions help explain what most people experience and where they are in the process. In order to live peacefully and happily, people need to find meaning in all three aspects of time and to make connections between these aspects.

In the table we have separated the spiritual issues from the religious resources in order to illustrate that persons who have no religious affiliation *do* have sspiritual tasks and resources. For those who have religious values, the spiritual and religious tasks and resources often are integrated.

Once again, we want to stress the importance of accepting people just as they are. Try not to inflict your own personal agenda, (which might be that you want the person to move through certain "phases" toward a particular psychological or spiritual place). You may have the knowledge and skill and understand that the person might need this or that, but your number one priority is to listen and to be a loving presence to a person facing loss or death.

THE PAST

Some persons are very reflective about their lives, while others go about their activities without giving much thought to meanings and connections.

Faced with the knowledge that death is imminent may place a person in a more reflective mode. The precious existence, once perhaps taken for granted, may be seen in a different light. Often, the person is drawn inward, leading to reflection on life's positives and negatives, joys and sorrows, regrets and satisfactions.

It is often beneficial for the dying to talk about their lives and to re-experience past events and the feelings that accompanied them. This review of their lives can bring closure and enable them to finish their business both on emotional and practical levels.

	Past	Present	Future
Spiritual Issues	Connect to the past Revive past support Express feelings about the past Seek forgiveness	Search for meaning Express feelings Make decisions about death	Find ways to leave a legacy and be remembered Move to sense of completion and letting go
Religious Resources	Rituals of reconciliation Prayer/Scripture/devotions	Sacraments/rituals/symbols Presence of faith community Prayer/Scripture/devotions	Hope in God's promise of resurrection life Hope in continuity of life through descendants

Table 7.1 The spiritual and religious aspects of ministry

One way to do this is to invite people to tell their stories. Many people respond positively to questions about life experiences, such as, "What was that like for you?" By asking such a question, you are asking for a description of feelings, which can help in telling the story. Because of telling their story, they often sense that their life is larger than what they are presently experiencing. They then may find a deeper meaning in both life and in their current reality.

The reflecting on the past can allow people to identify elements or resources that supported and enabled them to come through difficult times. These memories can give them strength and courage for the present. Sometimes people will talk about their failures and regrets to a caregiver who receives this reality "as is" and helps them express the feelings. The sharing of failures and regrets can lead to an inner healing. The past, when accepted, no longer controls the present.

Forgiveness of self and others is an important aspect of "living one's death." Churches offer many resources, for example, the Catholic church has a sacrament of reconciliation. This ritual celebrates God's enduring faithfulness and mercy made visible in the life, death, and resurrection of Jesus. While the act of confession of sins is done individually, it is also a community event. Churches, each in their own way, celebrate the reality that people are called to be a reconciling, forgiving, and faithful community of love. As a caregiver, you might help facilitate the expression of forgiveness by the dying person and those close to him or her. The forgiveness can be celebrated with whatever ritual is meaningful to them, with or without the help of a faith community.

The following are some Scripture passages that speak especially to the Christian person who is reviewing the past and is seeking God's forgiveness:

I have loved you with an everlasting love... (Jer 31:3)

No need to remember past events.
Look, I am doing something new (Is 43:18-19).

Unload your burden onto Yahweh,
and he will sustain you (Ps 55:22).

Then he said to her, "Your sins are forgiven" (Lk 7:48).

THE PRESENT

How a person feels about death depends largely upon the sense of meaning and faith the person lived. In order to be present to the dying, it is important to acknowledge your own mortality. Ask yourself, "What meaning does my life have at this point in time? What feelings do I have about my death? What is my image of death?" Because contemporary North American culture tends to deny death and dying, you may need to spend some time reflecting on the reality of your own death, using your imagination and then listening to and receiving whatever feelings come to you.

Our culture presents various images of death such as the "Grim Reaper," or an old hag. Images presented in the media sometimes shock and horrify. One fearful image is that of nothingness or non-existence. It frightens people and prompts them to wonder if their lives really have meaning.

In light of this fear, the Jewish belief in the continuation of life through the lives of descendants can be comforting and inspiring. Early Christians used images of rest, refreshment, and perpetual light. Images such as these are soothing and comforting and are still used in prayer: "Eternal light grant to her, O Lord, and let perpetual light shine upon her."

Just as images of death can vary, so too can ideas about God. The image a person holds most strongly of God will color that person's reaction to the reality of death. In other words, if a person's religious values emphasize God as a harsh, demanding judge, then the image of death and afterlife will most likely be fearful. On the other hand, if an individual is taught to view God as a loving, nurturing, and forgiving parent, then the person will probably look forward to being welcomed by and united with God. He or she will image death as "going home." For Christians, Jesus gives the image of heaven as a home:

In my Father's house there are many places to
live in; I am going now to prepare a place for you,
I shall return to take you to myself (Jn 14:2-3).

You may wish to invite people to talk about their images of
God and of death and their feelings associated with these
images. Sometimes through talking people will become more
aware of their personal experiences, understand God's touch
in their lives, and subsequently have their images be transformed and expanded.

Mary had been in the convalescent home for about three
years, and it became increasingly evident that her life would not
last much longer. Although she often mentioned her decreasing
strength and joked about death, she entertained no serious
discussion of those matters.

The staff took her, in her chair, to the daily devotions held in
the home. One day, Mary stopped the minister as he was leaving
the room and said, "Pastor Jethro, how can you have the nerve
to come here day after day and fill people's heads with this
garbage about a God who is a loving father and who will take
all of us to a wonderful home when we die? I have seen lots of
fathers, and most of them can hardly wait for their children to
get out of their sight. My father hated me and never did anything
kind. If that is what your God's love is like, I want nothing of
it! I got away from what my father called 'love' as soon as I could,
and I certainly don't want another father. Why don't you just
leave us all alone?"

The pastor was a wise man, and he did not argue with Mary.
Instead he told her that she had certainly given him something
to think about, and he thanked her. Then he spoke to the staff
who cared for Mary, asking them to always give her a choice
about whether she would attend the daily devotions. He knew
that one thing Mary longed for was the return of some control
over her own life.

On the days when Mary did not come to the service, Pastor
Jethro tried to stop into her room and spend a few minutes in
non-threatening, affirming conversation. One day, after about

six weeks of this practice, Mary suddenly said, "You know, Pastor, I'm dying."

At this point, Pastor Jethro was able to spend some time helping Mary share what that reality meant in her life. It turned out that not only was she worried about meeting a God who would personify her negative father image, but she was even more afraid of being reunited with the father she had known, who had been self-righteous and "religious" but also cruel to his wife and small daughter. The pastor was able to help Mary think about some other images of God and death. She soon began to recognize that God might turn out to be a gentle friend, as the pastor had been—someone who respected her and understood her fears.

Death often evokes fear of the unknown, but if the person comes to know God as a friend who can be trusted, the fear will often become less intense.

A dying person may sometimes ask questions in the search for meaning: "Why me?" or "What is the meaning of all this?" You cannot answer these questions. Even if you think you have some insights, they are the right ones for your life, not someone else's. Your task is to help the dying person find answers that mean something to that individual. You can facilitate this by being present, using good listening skills, and listening for inner meaning and purpose as the person tells her story. Your answers may not fit the person's experience, but your presence can help uncover answers that will be right and helpful.

As you are present to the person, attempt to facilitate the expression of such feelings as guilt, hopelessness, fear, anger, despair, depression, acceptance, joy, hope, and all the other emotions in the human spectrum. As you listen, you can help summarize recurrent themes or ideas, which in turn will help the person reflect upon what he has been saying. Such statements as "It sounds to me as if you've experienced a lot of pain in that relationship," or "That was a very joyous time," allow the person to reflect on and define his own feelings.

Sometimes music will help people touch their feelings and will bring forth comfort and healing during periods of suffering and loss. Music can communicate thoughts and feelings in ways that spoken words are unable. You can use different kinds of music, or ask people if they want to hear certain songs or compositions. If the person for whom you are caring is in a hospital, know that some hospitals offer music therapy, and you might choose to make a referral. If you do not work for the hospital, this simply involves sharing your observations and suggestions with the pastoral care chaplain or the head nurse on the unit.

Some dying persons wish to be involved in making decisions about their death, for example, deciding where they wish to die (at home, the hospital, the hospice unit, etc.) and who they want to have with them. When people can make their own decisions on these issues, they experience a sense of control, which increases their self-esteem. You need to be sensitive and careful not to push people into making these decisions if they prefer not to decide. Always try to accept people as they are. Understand also that there may be some dissent within families about these matters. For example, a person may wish to die at home, but the family may find this prospect frightening. Try to find the delicate balance between listening to the dying person and helping that person to understand the anguish of those who love him or her.

Religious Rituals

You as caregiver may suggest religious rituals and symbols if the dying person desires them; contact the appropriate members of the faith community to administer them. Many hospitals have departments of pastoral care or chaplains' services, which are there to help you with your ministry in any way they can. Contact these departments to coordinate your efforts with theirs. Offering religious or family rituals is one of their areas of expertise. For Christians these might include rites of forgiveness, or sacraments such as reconciliation and anointing of the sick.

Judaism

Jewish people are also encouraged, especially when death is approaching, to confess to God anything that may be burdening their hearts. They are also urged to beg pardon from any person they have hurt. This confession ritual is call *Vidui*, and although no specific person has to be present with the confessing person, you can suggest thinking of some person with whom it would be meaningful to share that moment—perhaps someone who has been especially supportive or someone whose pardon they wish to seek.

Traditionally a Jewish person near death will not be left alone. Jews believe that the soul may not leave the body while the person is alone. Loved ones must gather closely and observe death. This ritual is so important that ideally in the recitation of prayers over the dying person, the word "ONE" (the highest truth about God) must be said at the moment the soul leaves the body. (See Appendix A for the specific prayers connected with this ritual and for other Jewish practices at the time of death.)

Islam

Islam also provides near-death rituals that are meaningful to its believers. Iblis, the archangel rejected from Paradise and who, according to Islam, now reigns in the underworld, is believed to try to lure the dying person away from true faith by tempting the person with water to quench his thirst. Water or honey is placed on the tongue of the dying Muslim as an aid in resisting Iblis' offers. Similar to Judaism, when the time of death is thought to be near, a Muslim stays in the room and reads appropriate verses from the Koran.

Buddhism

The Buddhist moves toward acceptance of death by asking questions about the inevitability of death, and in the light of death, questions the meaning of life. Ideally, the Buddhist who is dying will be significantly detached from the people and possessions of this life so he can depart in peaceful preparation for rebirth.

This is why, if you are honored to be present at the last farewells of a Buddhist family, you may be surprised that a minimal emotion is displayed. Such display could distract the dying person from his peace, causing "excessive regret or longing"[1] and thus causing a less propitious rebirth. This special risk increases for persons who die in great emotional turmoil or shock, such as suicide.

The dying Buddhist's journey is mapped out with eight milestones or visions, which usually occur within the last few days before death as the body's organs fail. A teacher or close family member may stay with the dying person as a guide and support through this journey.

For religious people you may also like to suggest prayers, devotions, and readings that seem appropriate for that particular person. When these sacraments or rituals are celebrated, the presence of the faith community embodies God's love, acceptance, forgiveness, and care.

THE FUTURE

Dying persons usually think about the future in two ways. They think of what will happen after they die. Will they move on to some sort of eternal life, and, if so, what will that be like? They also think about the continuation of the meaning of their life on earth. The idea that something personal will continue to exist beyond their death can give meaning to the past and present. It can help to know that something of themselves, of their spirit or presence, will live on after they die. People often need to know that they have made a difference and will be remembered.

Be attentive for moments when dying persons or their families express these thoughts, and be sensitive to times when you might ask them about their feelings. The dying person and those close to him or her may wish to do something together to express this in a concrete way such as planning the funeral and burial services. There is a Jewish custom of naming a person after someone who has died, symbolizing the perpetuation of the meaning of the dead person's life. After World War II, some survivors of concentration camps actually took the names of those who had died so that those lives and deaths might have continued meaning.

There are many other ways to extend a person's presence beyond death. Some dying persons (and their families) make videotapes, audiotapes, picture collages. Others choose to leave a personal legacy by writing a song or a poem. Parents derive satisfaction from writing a letter or story for each of their children, who open the letters after the parent dies. Some families gather together with the dying person to share memories and to express their gratitude to this person for the gift her life has been to them. Activities such as these help people to ritualize and validate their grieving.

All these rituals help the dying person and those who love him or her to move toward a sense of completion and to let go. Like Bridget, the teen-ager in chapter four, many dying people need permission to die from the people closest to them.

> I (J.S.) have never forgotten an experience I had with a friend who was dying of cancer. She asked me to take her to the chapel, where we prayed together. Then she turned to me and asked, "Is it all right for me to die now?" We talked about it together and concluded that the time had come. She died shortly after that. It was important to her that she and I be consciously involved in this part of her journey.

Religious faith can give people hope, peace, and a sense of God's promise of new and everlasting life. For Jews, the Exodus story, and for Christians, the paschal mystery (the death and resurrection of Jesus) are strong affirmations of faith, life, and promise. We believe that for each person there is some meaning in life which can be tapped as a source of comfort and support. One of your main tasks as caregiver is to find that meaning and help the dying person and loved ones use it.

Chapter Eight

Prayer and Ministry

God, how can I conjure up the strength to continue going on? People tell me I'm strong—not really! You do what you have to—what else is there to do?

When I'm exhausted, I look around. There is no-one else but me.

People say it only happens to the strong. *Not true.* You do get strong because it has happened.

It won't destroy me. It might change me, though.

The ridiculous little worries of the past seem like a foreign language at this time. Every day, every hour that passes matters. Why couldn't I see that before?

Help me share his pain and make him well. Life can be beautiful. Thank you.

(Written in an intensive care waiting room by a woman whose husband was dying.)

Prayer is communication with God; it is the expression of a relationship. Human persons listen and speak to God and God also listens and speaks. It is simple yet profound, as in any

105

relationship. Everything discussed in chapter six about listening applies to the life of prayer.

To pray well, first of all you must listen to yourself and be open to your inner reality. This means being open to your own feelings and accepting them without judgment. You come to prayer as you are. This requires a commitment to really listen to your deepest self, to take time for intimacy with yourself, and to resist rushing into a superficial conversation with God. Your commitment to God is reflected in your commitment to personal honesty. With practice you can learn to become quiet and listen to your own experience and then to God.

In order to hear God speaking to your current situation, you can begin your prayer by listening to and naming what is going on inside you, inside your family, neighborhood, faith community, etc. It is into this reality that God often will speak to you. As you grow in your ability to listen and accept yourself, you will become more attuned and receptive to God's voice.

This listening stance requires that you become still. "Be still and acknowledge that I am God" (Ps 46:10). When you let go of "doing" and become quiet, you come to value yourself just as you are. This experience in itself prepares you for your own illness and death, the time when you will no longer have the satisfaction of achieving and accomplishing. These moments of stillness, quiet, and listening have the potential of uniting you in spirit with all people whose lives are now focused on "being" because their illness or incapacity prevents them from "doing."

God speaks in many ways—through nature, through events, people, religious services. Scripture is often one of the best ways to hear God's voice. By listening and receiving God's word, you can make it your own, a part of who you are. The Word of God nourishes, enlivens, and calls you forth in ministry. Isaiah says, "Listen, and you will live" (Is 55:3). When Ezekiel eats the scroll with the words of God, it tastes "sweet as honey"(Ez 3:3). And when God comes to Jeremiah, the word is given to empower the prophet to action:

> *Then Yahweh stretched out his hand and touched my mouth, and Yahweh said to me: "There! I have put my words into your mouth. Look, today I have set you over the nations, and kingdoms, to uproot and to knock down, to destroy and to overthrow, to build and to plant"* *(Jer 1:9-10).*

For Christians, Jesus sums up this call to ministry when he invites people to minister "for my sake, and for the sake of the gospel" (Mk 8:35). Your ministry flows out of and is nourished by your prayer.

COMPANION FOR THE JOURNEY

Your image of God affects your relationship with God and your prayer. Sometimes you may be unaware of your present image of God. It is beneficial to reflect on your life experiences and the images of God you have held. Ask yourself, "What is my image of God today?"

A person's image of God is often formed in childhood. For small children, the adults around them set the example for how they will experience God. For example, if their parents are distant, judgmental, controlling, or cruel, most children will think God is that way. Tender, sensitive parenting often enables children to open themselves to God's tender touch and to grow up with an understanding of unconditional love.

Many people grew up with an image of God as a stern and demanding judge. When people experience God this way they usually feel guilty and afraid, because they imagine that they do not measure up to God's expectations. Their prayers and their relationships with God are often calculating and measured, more "head" than "heart." This image also leads people to try to earn or merit God's love and favor.

No one can earn God's love. God's unconditional love is present regardless of what someone does or does not do. Prayer helps people become aware of the presence of this love. If God is imaged as a loving parent, the good shepherd, brother, or faithful friend, then prayer will more likely be tender and loving.

If you become aware of God's generous love and compassion for you personally, you will begin to pray with a longing to be filled by God. You will have less concern for your performance and how you measure up to God's demands. Your prayer will become more of a mutual presence.

The image of "companion for the journey" is often meaningful in ministry to people experiencing suffering and loss. We believe that this ministry would be difficult without the assurance that God is our companion, that this is God's work, and that it is God's love and compassion that touches others through us.

In turn, you are a companion in faith and love to others. Suffering persons often experience what they think is God's lack of response to their prayers for a cure or relief. Your loving presence and prayer may help them realize God's love once again. As they accept their lives, loss, and death, they can become more aware of God's faithfulness. Their prayer is often for God's continued companionship and for the reassurance that God will not abandon them. You are a living sign of God's companionship and love for them.

Many Scripture stories tell about companions on the journey, and you might prayerfully ponder these as you seek to identify what this companion image may mean to you personally.

For Christians, the Second Testament contains accounts of Jesus choosing the disciples, those who will follow him and assist him in his mission.

> *He made his way through towns and villages*
> *preaching and proclaiming the good news of the*
> *kingdom of God. With him went the Twelve, as*
> *well as certain women who had been cured of*
> *evil spirits and ailments (Lk 8:1).*

Tobit, one of the deuterocanonical books of the Bible, tells the story of a father who is dying and wants his son to go on a journey to recover the money that he had left with a friend (Tobit 5). The son, Tobias, does not know how to get to the place where the money is. He goes outside and finds a man whom he thinks is a brother Israelite. The man is actually Raphael, an angel of God. When Tobit asks him to go with his son, Tobias, Raphael replies,

> *"I shall complete the journey with him. Do not*
> *be afraid. On the journey outward all will be*
> *well; on the journey back all will be well; the road*
> *is safe" (Tob 5:20).*

By your prayerful and loving presence to persons who are on journeys of illness, loss, aging, death, or other human pain, you are like Raphael, the angel. Your faithful companionship assures people that all will be well and that the road is safe. Gradually, they may become more aware of God with them as a companion.

PRAYING WITH THE PERSON IN CRISIS

"The doctor just informed Joe and me that he has inoperable cancer. I can't believe it! How could God do this to us? We've just retired, bought a motor home, and have plans for many vacation trips."

You will hear statements like this when you go to visit someone facing a crisis or a terminal illness. At these times, people find it difficult to pray. They may express anger or disappointment in God and then feel guilty for having these feelings. Many people think it is wrong to be angry with God. However, since prayer is communication of a relationship, how can someone be wrong to communicate openly whatever he is experiencing? As with all relationships, people will occasionally experience conflict with God.

Each person's spiritual response to pain, loss, and grief will be different. Some people's faith will be deepened, some weakened. Some may feel a temporary paralysis of spirit—a nothingness. Some will be outraged by God. Others will feel closer to God than ever before.

Mary's husband died after they had been married for fifty-two years. She describes what she experienced in the months following her loss: "Everything seems trivial to me. I don't feel connected to anything." Jim experienced a deep crisis of faith when his wife died of cancer, leaving him with three young children. He was angry and felt abandoned by God. On the other hand, Julia, whose husband was killed in an auto accident, said she felt closer to God after the tragedy. She knew God's nearness and care for her; she felt God to be her constant companion.

You can help people express their feelings to God. You may first need to help them be aware of and name those feelings. People faced with serious illness and/or crisis will probably feel such emotions as frustration, anger, helplessness, fear, grief, abandonment, and hopelessness—all of which society has taught them to repress. In order to move from anger to peace, people need to express these feelings rather than deny them. Some people may find it helpful to draw or paint what they feel. For others, writing it out as a letter or prayer to God helps. You might refer them to places in Scripture where Jesus, the prophets, and the psalmist express their human emotions.

I waited, I waited for Yahweh,
then he stooped to me and heard my cry for help (Ps 40:1).

Shout for joy, daughter of Zion;
rejoice, exult with all your heart (Zep 3:14).

My soul is sorrowful to the point of death (Mk 14:34).

You have opportunities to pray with the grieving person and/or the family. Ask them if they would like to pray for some particular grace or gift. A simple way to help them touch God's presence is to ask them to remember times and places when they felt God's love for them. Or if you have heard their life story, reflect on the instances that stood out to you as manifestations of God's love.

As people of faith and prayer come closer to dying, their most satisfying form of prayer may be their peaceful awareness of God's presence with and love for them in their struggling, suffering, and letting go. As a caregiver you are privileged to be a sign to them of God's presence. Likewise, they are a sign to you of the prayer for companionship; you are journeying with them, being mutually enlivened, enriched, and deepened in God's faithful love.

Chapter Nine

Children and Death

Many people cling to a fantasy that does children a great disfavor. The fantasy is that children should always be happy, that childhood should be the happiest time of life—a time of being carefree and joyous. Yet even fairy tales, which have been told to children for generations, deny the fantasy of happiness and present pain and danger personified in witches, wolves, and trolls. Parents today are sometimes aghast to find such nasty creatures in fairy tales and refuse to tell the stories to their children. But these tales have survived the centuries precisely because they allow children to express their pain, their fears, their "forbidden reality." If told by a compassionate and wise adult, fairy tales can be a way for children to express what childhood is really like, helping adults remember long- forgotten realities which had been repressed in their own childhoods.

Childhood is, in fact, a time of happiness, but it is also a time of exploring the world. It is a time of being small and powerless and completely at the mercy of adult power figures. It is a time of struggling to understand that the reality of life doesn't line up with the ideals presented by the media. It is a time when an untethered imagination can help tell stories in poetic images that describe what a child is experiencing; it is a time when that same imagination can conjure images that are frighteningly worse than reality. Children need support, love, and guidance from people who are prepared to listen and learn from their experience. Finally, it is the time to learn about God, and the way to do that is to observe the behavior of significant adults. We believe that adults should not shield children from death. Rather, they should be available to listen to how their youngsters experience loss, to help them sort out their perceptions, and try to find answers that speak to their needs.

I (J.S.) attended the wake service for an elderly man. One of his granddaughters, a five-year-old, was sitting behind me next to her father. She was looking at the casket and asked her father, "Is that grandpa in there?" After her father said "Yes," she said, "Is that heaven?" Her father explained that only her grandpa's body was in the casket; the living part of him was in heaven. That response was sufficient for her.

Honest expressions and the words are important. Avoid using euphemisms, which confuse children. If you do not speak directly and openly, if you avoid the words "dead" and "death," children may consider death a forbidden subject and repress their thoughts and feelings. Children also interpret words literally. For example, you need to be careful not to refer to someone who has died as "asleep." This evokes fear in children: if the they or the persons they love go to sleep, it might result in death.

Many children attend some sort of religious education classes where they hear stories of a loving God, perhaps personified in Jesus. This God is in some other celestial place, and because children visualize concrete images for nearly everything, they literally believe in heaven as a place that is up and hell as down. Because everything exists in the present for children, and everything centers on "me", they relate well to the idea that God is personally interested in how they live their lives and whether or not they are good or bad boy and girls. Children often see a direct relationship between their own behavior and everything that happens around them. They regard outer events as reward or punishment for their behavior. (How often do adults themselves ask, "What did I do to deserve this?") Death is an event that most children take personally.

DEATH OF A PET

For many children, their first experience with death is the death of a pet.

Buffy, the Rodriguez' pet dog, was killed on the road. He had escaped from the yard when someone did not latch the gate securely, although nobody knows who was responsible. The three children in the family each responded differently to the loss.

Maria, who was twelve, wanted to go to the city offices to collect Buffy's body. She held the stiff little form in her arms and crooned a soft song of love. Then she insisted that her parents purchase a plot in a pet cemetery and hold a burial ceremony, which she designed and orchestrated. She was sad in a ritualistic sort of way for a week, and then she didn't talk much more about Buffy or his death. But for about a year, whenever her parents took her to that part of town, she spent a few minutes thinking about Buffy at the pet cemetery. About six months after Buffy's death, she asked for another pet.

Jason, the seven-year-old, was quiet for several hours after learning of Buffy's death. He refused to go to the burial service that Maria held, and he left the room whenever others spoke about the little dog. He picked fights with his sisters for several days and would not respond when his parents called him until they came to look for him. He spent hours in his bedroom with the door closed, coloring pictures he would not show to anyone. For three weeks he would not go to church. He was very angry.

One day, Jason shouted at his mother for something completely unimportant, then he ran to his room and slammed the door. After a few minutes, his mom followed and found Jason lying with his face in his pillow. When she pulled him into her arms, he sobbed and sobbed. Jason was having many frightening feelings about Buffy's death. He blamed himself because he had often left the gate open and been scolded for it. He was very angry with the driver who had hit his pet and left him in the road to die. He was angry with his parents, who were powerless to bring Buffy back, and with himself for the same reason. He thought that his sister's ceremony contributed to "making Buffy stay dead." Deep inside, he was afraid that if Buffy had died so easily and so quickly, so might some of the people Jason loved—maybe even Jason himself.

Once Jason had poured out his pain to his mother, she could help him sort out his thoughts and feelings, and he went on his way back to happiness and contentment. When Maria's new puppy arrived, she allowed her brother to name it. For Jason, that was the last necessary rite for dealing with his pain.

The Rodriguez' youngest daughter, Martha, was only four years old. When Maria and her father went to the city offices to claim Buffy's body, Martha insisted on going along. On the way, she displayed great excitement. As her sister cradled Buffy's body and sang to him, Martha sat to one side with a puzzled expression on her face. In the car, she reached over and touched the blanket-covered body and asked, "Is this really Buffy?"

That evening, Martha went about her life as usual. Next morning, she asked, "Can we go and get Buffy now?" When her parents replied that Buffy was dead, she said, "I know that, but when is Buffy coming home?" She attended the burial rite that Maria conducted, and she wept a bit when Maria told her to put a flower on the little box and say, "Good-bye, Buffy." But the next day she again asked for her pet to come home. In her prayers each day, she asked Jesus to "Make Buffy better. Make his back not be broken so he can walk again." She peacefully insisted that it was just a matter of time before Jesus would heal Buffy and bring him back. Over time, she mentioned her pet less and less, until her family thought that she had forgotten. But the day the new puppy arrived, she watched his baby steps across the kitchen. Then she bent down, picked him up, and said, "Buffy can't come back, can he? Buffy's dead and can't come back," she said as she hugged the new puppy.

Each child in this family experienced the loss of their pet in a different way. Each of their expressions of the loss reflected their personalities and also their ages.

Little Martha could not understand how someone she loved could not be alive. She had seen cartoon characters terribly battered one moment and alive the next. At Sunday school, she had learned how Jesus healed various sick people. She had put the two ideas together and figured out that Jesus was the magic ingredient in hurt people getting well again. She could not visualize death, a state quite removed from her own experience.

As time passed, Martha's attention span for the loss shortened, and she moved on to new life adventures. But somehow, the questions remained in her mind. By the time the new puppy arrived, Martha's mind had come up with the logical answer, "If someone is gone for a long, long time, they will not come back. That is what 'dead' means." The sight of the new pet brought that conclusion to the surface. Martha had not worked out any deep theological or philosophical theory of death; she had found an answer that worked for her. "Death means someone has gone away for such a long time that you know they are not coming back."

Jason, however, at the age of seven, already knew that death was both something permanent and something to be feared. He had seen people in movies hanging from buildings or running from other fates that meant death. He knew that death was painful, and he knew something or someone caused it. Now he learned that death didn't just happen in the movies but could attack someone he loved. He found the whole thing very frightening, and he hoped that somehow he could avoid talking about it long enough to make it not real. (Many adults also play this game.) When this ploy didn't work, he felt helpless and vulnerable, and anger accompanied those feelings, which frightened him even more. Jason was confused, but his parents had wisely waited until he was ready to talk about his confusion and fear rather than pressing him to cheer up before he was ready.

Twelve-year-old Maria understood death. At school, a classmate's mother died, and the class had talked about what that meant. To her, the loss of an animal was as important as the loss of a parent, and she wanted to acknowledge that importance. Her reaction and ritual were healthy, and her parents were wise to encourage her to express her grief constructively. Only a few months later, Maria's grandmother died, and she was able to stand in front of the congregation and sing a hymn her Grandma had loved. That was not easy, but somehow, even at her young age, Maria understood that ritually expressing pain can greatly facilitate healthy and constructive grieving and can move a person toward life again.

Just as these three children each faced the death of a pet in different ways, so too will children react differently to the death of a real person. For children, a pet is a "significant other." Parents are wise to let children grieve for the loss of a pet and not try to cheer them up too soon with a replacement animal. Grieving for pets is excellent preparation for grieving the loss

of human loved ones who sometimes die before children are grown. They can then say, "I remember when Champ died. That really hurt a lot. But it did get better, and now I can think of Champ without that terrible pain. If I am patient and allow my parents to help me, I know that I can learn not to hurt so much every time I think of Grandpa."

PARENT, GRANDPARENT, OR ANOTHER CHILD

Children know that other children are like themselves in special ways. Even a baby shows excitement and pleasure when another small person arrives, as if to say, "Oh good, someone else who is small like me!" They feel a common bond and kinship with each other, which grownups cannot share.

The death of a parent or grandparent is confusing and painful, and children need both patient support and love. But the death of another child, especially a sibling, is devastating. Children are egocentric; they think the world revolves around them. If an adult or a pet dies this will frighten them, but because they identify so strongly with another child, a child's death is the most frightening of all. They sometimes are so personally threatened and confused by this death that they may not even know how to verbalize their fear. With time and patience, a caring helper can assist them in articulating what this death means to them. This requires much skill, and also an interest, since a child's grief can be like following a frustrating maze into unexplored country. It is a special gift when a child trusts an adult enough to share something as intimate as pain and fear. Only certain adults have the ability to elicit this trust. If you know a child who is grieving, and if you find yourself unable to touch the core of that experience, you may need to accept help from a person with that special ability.

If you want to enter the child's world of grief, one way to help children express what they are feeling is to invite them to draw a picture. (See figure 9.1 for the drawing mentioned in the following story.)

Christina was a five-year-old girl just about to enter kindergarten. Her father died suddenly in front of his family at breakfast.

Christina did not seem terribly upset over the loss, although she did become whiny and demanding as her mother struggled for enough energy to manage single parenting. Since Christina had always been closer to her mother, her family simply assumed that she did not miss her father too much; they figured her demanding behavior was caused by the changes in family routine.

About six months after the father's death, I (D.R.W.) was asked to spend some time with Christina because she was having stomach problems and was refusing to eat. She claimed eating caused her pain.

I had previously developed a friendship with this little girl, sensing that she would probably need help sometime in the future. Now that she was obviously upset, I had no trouble

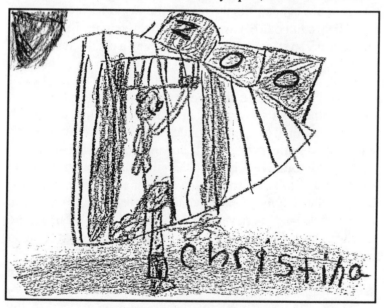

Figure 9.1. Christina's drawing

communicating with her. I talked to her about how her daddy's death had come right at the time she was starting school, and that lots of boys and girls found starting school difficult even with two live parents. She agreed. But now, I explained, school wasn't so hard anymore because she had figured out how things worked. Yet something strange was happening to her tummy. She nodded gravely.

"Christina, do you think very often about your Daddy? Do you remember when he was with you?"

"Yes. I think about how we went places. I dream about him, too."

"What do you dream?"

"I dream about him here, and then I dream that he isn't here."

I explained to Christina that her dreams and her tummy problem both occurred because her body was trying to help her understand how sad she really felt inside. I asked her to get her crayons and paper and draw me a picture of how she felt. The picture she drew was not sad; I asked her to explain how it showed her feelings.

"The sunshine shows my happy feelings. This is a picture of a little girl at the zoo. There is a monkey in the cage."

"What sort of feelings are in the monkey, Christina?"

"The monkey is happy and playing and joking. That is how I am sometimes."

"But the monkey is in a cage. Is that how your funny, playful feelings are?"

"Yes. That is how I feel. The little girl looking at the monkey is my cousin, Sara. She is lonely because someone she loves is far away."

Sensing that "Sara" was really Christina, I continued, "The ground is black in your picture, Christina. What does the ground stand for?"

"The ground is the little girl's tummy. It hurts and it feels like someone is walking on it. It is black."

"Christina, I wonder if that little girl could really be you. It seems to me that her tummy hurts just like yours."

After a thoughtful pause, she said, "I think she is me. Sara is lonesome, but I am lonesome too, for Sara and for my Grandpa and for my Daddy. My tummy really hurts."

"I am glad that you understand so much about yourself. You are a very smart girl. I notice that the cage covers part of the little girl. Is she standing in front of it, or is she partly inside it?" The cage was thick and black.

"I think she is watching the funny monkey, and she doesn't know what is the key to let him out of the cage. She wants him to get out, but she can't find the key." All this from a child!

"Christina, I think that maybe the key to letting out those happy, funny feelings is to share with other people—people you can trust such as your mom or me—about how you are feeling. What do you think?"

"I feel real sad. I don't want my daddy to be dead."

For this child, drawing her feelings and talking about the picture was the beginning of understanding what she was experiencing. Once she understood, she felt less need to run from her reality.

Even without analyzing their works of art, both adults and children can often help themselves just by creating. If you are caring for a grieving child, be sure that they have several media, such as crayons, paint, and modeling clay, to work through their experiences. Most parents are happy to supply these materials, but you may need to encourage them to offer their children means of expressing themselves visually.

Whenever you find yourself touching the life of a grieving child, keep in mind these three facts:

1. Children are people. When things go wrong, they are just as much affected as adults. Do not assume that they should always be happy.
2. What children perceive and experience in a situation may differ from what adults around them perceive and feel. Find a way to enable children to tell you *their* unique experiences.
3. Take children seriously, and they will more readily communicate their feelings with you.

CARING FOR THE PARENTS

The words "child" and "death" do not seem to fit together. People do not like to think about the "premature" death of a child. For parents, the death of a child is usually the most frightening idea they can imagine. Parents are totally invested not only in the reality of their children's presence in their lives but also in their vision of their children's futures and the children's continuation in life after the parents' death. Just the thought of the lost potential is unspeakably painful.

The loss of a child is one of the worst possible grief experiences. Everything explained in this book, all of the symptoms and needs of those who mourn, may be magnified in those grieving for a child. The incidence of marital break-up nearly doubles when a child dies.

Many caregivers do not know how to relate to this pain. Sometimes a child's death challenges people to examine their personal fears and reflect upon their own pain. Because of this, caregivers often move away emotionally from the mourners and make little effort to support them beyond superficial expressions of condolence. Parents whose children have died express feeling "frozen out," neglected, ostracized, like an embarrassment to their communities and their faith families. They also say that after the first couple of weeks (when the numbness has worn off and the pain becomes intense) no one comes to visit.

If the parents feel guilty in some way for the death (and the vast majority do feel this way), they often interpret this neglect as a judgment. They mistakenly think that the community is ostracizing them because people judge them responsible for the death and believe that they were "bad" parents in some way.

One extremely important reassurance to give to such parents,in fact, to any parent who loses a child, is that you believe in them *as parents*. There are many ways to do this. Offer your ongoing support and show them you validate their continuing grief. You might call or visit on special days, days when you imagine shadow grief (see p. 65) will bc strong. Help parents talk through their pain or suggest a project such as a memory book about the child's life. Encourage them to join a support group with other people who are experiencing similar pain. Invite them gradually back into community activities and life. Let them know, however you can, that they are still loved and valued.

Addictive, Mental, or Emotional Illness

For some parents, one painful grief experience is the loss of a teen-ager or young adult to addictive diseases or to other mental or emotional illnesses. Many consider this a death, and indeed it is the death of the idealized picture of success nurtured by Western society. A parent must accept their child as wounded, fallible, and capable of seriously unacceptable behavior. Compounding the problem, the child must often be hospitalized, and the parents' visiting rights may be limited and controlled.

"I remember what it was like," one mother recalls. "Two big male nurses came out into the hospital foyer and took my son away. His last looks at me were a heartbreaking combination of anger and agony. They disappeared through double doors, and I heard them turn the keys in the locks. Then I was alone in the lobby, and my other son came and led me away. I could not have driven myself home. The tears were streaming down my face. Behind my tears, I just kept seeing his sweet face when he was a little boy. I remembered how he would cling to me when he was afraid. I felt as if I had lost my son, and I wasn't sure if I could get to know this new personality, or even if he wanted to ever see me again. I have never felt so much pain or so much confusion."

Whatever the situation to which you are called, always respond with extreme love and care, and with prayer. God, the loving parent, will guide you in this tender ministry.

Children with AIDS

One painful struggle becoming more common is the struggle of the parents of a child dying with Auto-Immune Deficiency Syndrome (AIDS). This may be either an adult child or a young person.

Unfortunately, Western society labels persons with AIDS with many cultural taboos because of the ways in which the virus is most often spread. Although a *person with AIDS* (PWA) may have been infected through invasive medical techniques, by far the majority have become ill directly because of sexual behaviors or drug use. These people have often been alienated to varying degrees from their families because of their lifestyles.

When the child becomes terminally ill, the family must deal not only with the reality of approaching death but also with the pain that has existed between them. This pain is due to disapproval, values, pride, and a great many other factors. The work with these families is one of the most difficult areas of grief support.

One question in the minds of many parents of a PWA is, "What did we do wrong? Did we drive our child into the lifestyle that caused the infection?" So that you can respond in constructive ways to these concerns, take time now to read some current literature on the sources of both addictions and homosexuality. One of the most healing things you can do is to help parents understand that their child is a worthwhile person, beloved by God.

It is vital that you as a caregiver become aware of your personal reactions to the value-laden implications of this disease. Ask yourself, "How do I feel about the lifestyle that has led to this person's becoming infected with AIDS? Am I really able to put aside society's judgments and respond to the needs of this family?"

It is also important that you examine your own feelings about being near people with infectious diseases. If you cannot bring yourself to touch or embrace the sick person (if you obviously rush to wash your hands off after each encounter), then the words of affirmation you speak will have no value. Both the infected person and the family will translate your actions not into concern about infections but into concern about the value of the person who is infected. Learn about AIDS. Understand that you *will not* become infected from touching or embracing a PWA. Learn also when and how you should be careful.

> Mr. S. was dying of AIDS. His liver had stopped functioning and he was hemorrhaging from his nose and mouth. His wife and son had been sitting with him for several days, and one morning they asked me (D.R.W.) about bringing his teen-age grandchildren to "say good-bye." They did not want to tell the young people that their grandfather had AIDS.
>
> Usually, I would have agreed that the family carry out their plan as they saw fit. But in this case, because of the blood that was flowing from Mr. S.'s body, and because of the reality that his grandchildren should wear gloves and be wise about embracing him, I advised the family that the young people should know the truth.
>
> I offered my support in telling them, but I insisted that, if they come in the room, they must know the reality.

Supporting families wherein AIDS has occurred requires a great deal of non-judgmental love and a conviction in the goodness of all people. If you are not able to do this, it is best to refer the family to someone who can. These parents need to be able to see their child's strengths and good points and to feel strong about their own parenting. You will have to emphasize these positive factors in the face of many other people who say the opposite. Take time to examine your own heart to find out if you can do this.

CARING FOR THE DYING CHILD

The other side of the coin is to care for a child suffering from a fatal illness. Confusion and fear usually govern the actions of adults in this situation, who suffer the frustration of seeing pain (both physical and mental) they cannot remove. They question whether or not to tell the child that he or she is dying.

Medical people themselves sometimes do not even know if they should tell the parents. It is difficult for doctors to tell parents that they, the professionals to whom the care of the child has been entrusted, cannot make the child well. One reason it is difficult is that often the child will be removed from the diagnosing physician's care because the parents seek other opinions and alternative treatments. Another reason for hesitancy is that the anger of the parents as they grieve may be focused on the doctor. Finally, the doctor may even go through a kind of self-castigation because he or she is trained to defeat death and is losing the battle.

Many parents, in their need to deny the obvious, facilitate the denial of medical professionals and other helpers. Children on the other hand, are much more honest, and even the younger ones will ask amazingly astute questions about their own prognoses. They know they are sick, and they sense they may die. They know that some important people are avoiding telling them the truth, and that increases their pain.

Linda was ten years old. For three years, she had struggled with leukemia, which had gone into remission for a few months and then returned with a vengeance. Now, her tiny body exhausted. She lay in the big hospital bed, her face turned to the wall. The chaplain was called to see her because of her "depression." In other words, I (D.R.W.) was called in to cheer up a dying child.

Outside Linda's room I met her mother. She looked exhausted. She had not left the hospital for days, changing clothes in the restroom. Friends did her laundry and baby-sat her other child so that she could be with Linda. I sat with her for a few minutes, and she gave me the impression of someone whose emotions were completely drained away.

"You seem very tired and seem to have hardly any feelings left," I said. "Is that because you have been hurting so much, for so long, that you feel drained? Or, is it because you are holding all your emotions inside so you won't upset Linda?" (I was trying to enable her to assess her own situation, something she likely would not have done on her own because all her energy was being used in simply getting by.)

"For all these months and years, I have been trying to take care of myself because we didn't know how long this would go on. Now, when we are nearing the end...(a long pause, as she obviously gathered herself together)...I can't seem to deal with it. If Linda is sleeping, I can stay with her. But as soon as she wakes up and looks at me, I break down and have to leave the room."

"Why do you leave the room when you cry? Does it upset your daughter to see that you are sad?"

"I don't know; she has never seen me cry. I don't want to take the chance."

"Are you telling me that, in three years of sharing all the treatments and pain and indignities, you and Linda have never cried together?"

"That's right." A proud look came over her face. "I have always waited till I was alone."

"Has Linda ever cried?"

"Of course, whenever the treatments were painful or she felt sad, I have always been there for her. Her father and I are divorced, and he doesn't like to come to the hospital. It hurts him too much."

"So in all this time, Linda has never really seen you show your agony? She has never had any real sign that you were sad when she was ill?"

Proudly, "No."

"If Linda were not going to die, if she simply had a very miserable, uncomfortable chronic disease, would you still be sad?"

"Of course."

"If she were going to live a long life, would you be able to share your pain with her and not be so afraid of upsetting her?"

Thoughtfully, "I think so. I wouldn't have to face the questions in her eyes."

At that moment I remembered that this woman could sit with her daughter when the child's eyes were closed in sleep. I also remembered that the nurses had told me that Linda was lying with her face to the wall.

"Mrs. K., I think your daughter knows how you are struggling, and she is trying to help you by not making you look into her eyes and not asking questions. When they are ill, many young children sense they might die. Like you and me, they really don't know what that means. They need to explore their feelings and ask questions about what happens after death, just like we would if it were us. Children also need to see certain people to say, 'Good-bye.' I imagine that if Linda's father is staying away, that could be worrying her a lot.

"If a child sees the adults around them expressing their emotions, it is very freeing. It gives a child the permission to express any fears she might be having.

"I can understand that you have had to take care of yourself over the last few years and not use up all your emotional energy prematurely. But you don't have to do that anymore. This is the time you have been waiting for, and this is the time for honest sharing. I believe that is the best thing for both Linda and yourself.

"I will go in to visit with Linda to make sure that I am not wrong in my conclusions, but if I still believe that Linda wants you to relax and cry with her and wants to have you near her, even if you are upset, are you willing to try?"

The mother had been listening carefully, and since she wanted to do what was best for her daughter, she agreed to try.

After introducing myself to Linda, I sat beside her bed, talking to her back.

"Linda, I really would like to know what is happening with you today. The nurses tell me you are feeling sad."

"You know what's happening."

In a low voice, I slowly said, "Actually, I don't. I have just met you, and I'm not a doctor. But I can see that you are sick, and I know that you have been for a long time. That must sometimes make you scared, maybe a little confused. I know that if it were me, I would feel that way. Is that how you feel?"

After several minutes of silence, Linda said, "I'm pretty sure that I'm dying."

It is always a bit of a shock to hear such a mature statement come from such a small person.

"Why do you think that?"

"Well...I have been real sick since I was seven years old. I got better in grade three but then I got sick again in the summer. And they don't give me the chemo anymore. They just give me things to make it stop hurting when my bones or my head aches...Any my daddy doesn't come anymore. I think he is too sad. My mommy runs out of the room and cries and if she thinks I am asleep, she stays here. She thinks I am ugly now, so I try not to let people see my face."

"Linda, let me look at your face, please. I will tell you honestly if you are ugly. Then we can figure out if that is really what is bothering your mom."

Slowly she turned over. I was careful not to show any shock at seeing the emaciated little face. I gradually smiled at her.

"You are not at all ugly. You are very thin, but you still look like a sweet girl. I am sure that is not what keeps your parents away. Let's try to figure out what the real problem might be."

When she knew that I would really try to help her with her emotional turmoil, Linda opened up to me. It was not difficult from that time on, to bring her mother to the point of holding Linda and allowing them both to cry. Getting the father to the hospital was more difficult, but before Linda's death (the next week) the three of them had sat together and shared memories. The parents shared some of those memories at the funeral, and I could hear her small voice saying, "Remember the time we went to the picnic at Smithers' Beach...."

Linda's story illustrates what we have found time and again: children are people, and all people deserve enough honesty to give them a sense of control over their own lives. If children are lied to (and avoidance is a type of lie), then they may imagine things that are worse than reality. They become frightened when people they want to trust obviously lie to them. It sometimes takes an experienced helper to share truth with children in a way they can understand and at a level they can accept.

Chapter Ten

The Death of a Baby

Few losses are so painful to contemplate as the death of a baby, because babies are so full of potential for the future. When a child is born, every promise ever made to humanity by God once again becomes possible. In the presence of newborns adults often feel young again. When a baby smiles, something melts within the hardest heart. Birth signifies continuation; parents hope their children will carry on their names and traditions and in turn pass them on to their own children.

A tiny child is completely vulnerable and completely dependent on adults for its very life. Parents feel a sense responsibility. When a baby dies, caregivers themselves often feel a sense of "if only...," and wonder if they could have somehow prevented it. A natural sense of guilt adds to the desolation of grief.

One question many parents of sick babies have is, "Why is God punishing my child like this?" They may articulate the question in different words, but it all stems from the idea that God is, somehow, causing their child's suffering—perhaps because of some sin on the parent's part.

You as caregiver must try to respond to this question. You can help the parents to examine their own image of God. Why the baby is sick or dying is a mystery. While the reality is that

there are bad things in this world, and that these bad things often
hurt good people, God does not cause this to happen. God only
loves the little baby.

YOUR FEELINGS AS CAREGIVER

The call to care for parents whose children have died comes
too often to every faith community. If you are a parent yourself,
you may find responding to this situation particularly difficult.
Before going examine your own feelings; they may be very
strong. If you understand *your* feelings, you will be more sensitive to the parents' feelings and needs.

Anger is an emotion people commonly feel when a baby dies.
Sometimes people ask, "How could God allow this to happen?"
When they ask this question, they often mean, "Why did this
happen? Who do I blame? Please help me find that I can still
worship God and know that God loves me even though my child
is gone. Help me believe God cares."

These questions are difficult to verbalize, and people seldom
ask them point blank. Your task is to intuit what the real issues
are. Sometimes, parents lash out at God and as a result, you may
be threatened by this; after all, you (if you are the minister from
the faith community) may represent God in this situation. Try
to remember that anger is a normal expression of grief, and
focusing anger on God is also normal and usually temporary. If
you let their anger affront you, you might only confirm in their
minds that God really does not care enough to receive their
anger and pain.

I (D.R.W.) was called to the pediatric intensive care unit
because the doctors were about to tell a couple that their
two-year-old daughter was brain dead and should be removed
from life support. The child had been injured in an accident the
day before.

I sat and listened as the doctors very gently told the parents
that there was no possible way their little girl could live and that
the best thing for her was to let her go. The parents asked for

some time to think, and the doctors left. I sat quietly, asking myself, "What can anyone possibly say right now that won't make the pain worse?" I decided to let them take the lead. After a few minutes, the father spoke straight to me in a harsh voice. "They want us to 'let her go.' Go to who? To a God who let this happen, let a drunk woman hit her and run her over, let my little girl, our baby, lie there with no brains left? What kind of a God would do that?" He broke down into sobs.

I moved over, knelt beside his chair, and put my arm around his shoulder. He pulled away. I stayed beside him, only gently touching his arm with my hand.

"Mr. Jeffries, I can never understand how deep this pain must be for you, because this has never happened to me. However, one of my nightmares is that one of my children will be hurt in this way, so I have a bit of an idea of what it must feel like. I can see your beautiful little girl lying in the bed, and it makes me angry. No matter how many times I see this happen, I still get mad, more so when stupidity is the cause. I know that if the woman had been sober, the accident never would have happened, and I find that so frustrating! Here in the hospital, we witness these senseless tragedies too often, and I have asked myself the same question as you did. I work for this God. Do I want to go on working for a God who allows such abominations?

"There are no easy answers. But I would like to tell you that I have learned that God has very little to do with these things, nor does God will them. I have sensed over and over again that these tragedies make God just as sad and angry as they do us. I know, without a doubt, that God is weeping right now for your little girl."

Mrs. Jeffries had been silent until this time, lost in her own thoughts. Now she spoke quietly. "How can I let her go? She's my baby. I can't live without her. How can I let her go?"

I moved toward her and cradled her in my arms. She did not pull away. Her husband was listening to her weep but did not physically move toward her.

The mother continued, "Maybe, if I had been closer to her, she wouldn't have been hit. I might have seen the car coming.

I never expected a car to be coming through the park. I just didn't think of that. I thought we were safe."

Recognizing that this was normal self-questioning, I did not try to deny the questions or push them away.

"Everyone who loses a child has questions like yours. There are no answers, but it is good that you can ask the questions. We know that you are a good mother. You have been here at the hospital every minute, loving Jennifer and caring for her. I am sure that you were looking after her well when this happened. This is one of those things no one can prepare for because no one thinks it will happen. *You are a good mother.*"

We all sat in silence for a while, then I said, "Mr. and Mrs. Jeffries, you are very good parents. One of the hardest tasks for parents is letting children go after they are grown. You won't even have the chance to watch Jennifer grow. That makes it much harder for you than for most parents. I don't think the doctors were trying to be cruel; they are really thinking of what's best for Jennifer. She has suffered for twenty-four hours, and she tried very hard to live. But now she is at the point where she *can't* live; her little body is just too hurt. You can see that; you told me last night that her face doesn't even look like Jennifer anymore.

"Jennifer is so important to you that you can't imagine your life without her. I don't even want you to try to imagine what it will be like. But I do want you to think about what Jennifer needs now. You are her loving parents, and only you can make that decision. What does she need now?"

They both slowly raised their heads and looked at each other. The husband reached out and took his wife's hand. For several minutes they just looked into each other's eyes. The depth of their pain and love filled the room.

Finally Mr. Jeffries spoke. "We need to let her go." There was strength and surety to his voice.

"But," said the mother, "can we spend some time with her first?"

I assured them that they could have as long as they needed, and I left the cubicle. About twenty minutes later, I peeked in. They both were sitting beside Jennifer, stroking her. Their tears fell on her chest. Mr. Jeffries indicated that they were ready, and the doctors removed the life support equipment. During the few minutes it took for Jennifer's heart to stop beating, they took turns holding her in the rocking chair and singing nursery rhymes and old hymns that she had loved.

Several weeks later, the couple returned to the hospital to thank the staff for our compassion. They told us that the time they had spent saying good-bye to Jennifer was one of their special memories of her.

Sometimes it helps to compare parents' misplaced anger with that of teen-agers. Teen-agers, while working through all the crises of that stage of life, are often confused and hurt. But teens don't show that pain to their peers because their peers might judge them and turn away. Instead, adolescents come home and yell at their parents. If you, as God's minister, find yourself receiving anger that is meant for God, ask yourself how that loving parent would react to the situation.

I (D.R.W.) can remember when my daughter was a teen-ager; I would listen to the way she closed the door in order to learn what sort of mood she was in. By listening to the door, I had some idea of what to expect when she spoke to me. I was often tempted to be hurt when she flew off the handle at me for some minor matter. I had to remind myself that her exhibition of anger with me was actually a compliment (though one I could have cheerfully done without). She knew that I would not stop loving her, no matter what she said or did. She would sometimes really test my love to the limit, but it was through this sort of relating that she came to understand something of God's unconditional love.

KINDS OF DEATH

Miscarriage, Spontaneous Abortion, Stillbirth

People easily sympathize with the pain of a couple whose infant dies from Sudden Infant Death Syndrome (crib death) or in an accident. Likewise, when a baby is severely ill, relative and friends flock to support the parents at the hospital. But when a couple loses a child to miscarriage, spontaneous abortion, or stillbirth, people often lack sensitivity. Some tell couples not to grieve because "You are young and you'll have more children." Others advise couples to get pregnant again soon, as if another pregnancy could erase the loss of the dead child. Many people don't mention the loss at all and act as if the pregnancy hadn't existed. Others stay away because they don't know what to say.

As soon as a couple knows that a baby is growing inside the woman, they begin to emotionally acknowledge and to love the baby. They build a dream around the future of the child. When the pregnancy prematurely terminates, so too does the dream. To make matters worse, unlike the couple who can remember the child, these parents have no photographs or memories —only empty arms and a world that acts like their child had never been conceived. Some parents worry about what people will think if they talk about their dead baby. You can help these couples by encouraging them to talk, both about their pain and about their baby. They might want to hold the dead infant, if it is formed enough, and to name their child.

You can free them by recognizing that their child was alive and that they are *good* parents. If they are people of faith, assure them that although God wanted them to have a child, the baby was too ill to be born. You might say, "God took your baby and is holding him (or her) close right now."

Never call the baby "it." If they do not know what the baby's gender was, ask them if they would like to imagine which sex their child was. Creating an identity for their child can be healing. They can also refuse a naming or identifying ritual if they wish. Nothing should ever be forced on the parents. Suggesting ways to ritualize the baby's death may help, since they may not know that to need these symbolic actions is acceptable and will assist their grief.

Offer the parents the opportunity to see and hold the deceased child and assure them that to do so is normal and healthy. Leave the choice up to them, but you might tell them that other parents in a similar situation sometimes come back six months later to say that it was meaningful and they are happy they did it. (On the other hand, some parents would be horrified to see their child's dead body. This practice is dimly viewed in some cultural groups, and for such people the experience would not facilitate the grieving and would be unhealthy.)

Death of a Newborn Child in the Hospital

Even with all the advances in neonatal technology, many children still die shortly after birth. Most hospitals today recognize the need of the parents to bond with their baby for the short period of time available. If you are the caregiver in this situation, you may need to insure that the parents are being allowed this right.

Usually high-risk newborns are whisked immediately after birth into the Neonatal Intensive Care Unit (NICU). There they are connected to life support equipment, and tremendous efforts are made to sustain their lives. Often the main problem is that the child's premature lungs have not had enough gestational time to develop fully; if a machine can breathe for the child for some time, the lungs may mature. This tenuous procedure has many problems and risks, and the parents will be well aware that their baby is very, very fragile.

Parents are usually welcome in NICU to touch and bond with their baby. This is fine if the child lives for several days, but sometimes an infant is very near death, and the medical personnel will continue to monitor its progress.

As a caregiver in this situation, if the parents have not spent time with the baby, you can ask to speak with the physicians or nurses in charge. Explain that you are trying to respond to the parents' needs, and ask the medical team to give you some idea of the child's prognosis. If they say that the baby is not going to live, ask them if it is possible to disconnect the life support system so that the parents can hold their child for a short while before death. Most physicians and nurses will be happy to cooperate with this plan. (Because it may not be their usual procedure, they may not have thought of it themselves.)

The medical people are interested in the feelings of the parents, but their main concern is for the infant. They are trained to fight until the last moment to save that baby's life. You should approach them with courtesy and respect, explaining your concern while asking for their help.

If a child has a chance to live, it will be connected to so many tubes and bottles that the parents may have trouble emotionally ac cepting their baby. Talk to them about this. Encourage them that their voices and touch are more important to their child than anyone else's. They may be afraid to bond emotionally with their baby because they think that will make the pain worse if the baby dies. You can say something like, "Other couples have said that they were bitterly sorry they didn't spend more time with their children before they died. They wish they had more memories of touching their babies. Also, your baby needs to know that you are near, right now. Even if he will have a short life, he needs to feel your love, and your touch and voice are what will communicate that love." Many parents just need some encouragement.

After a short time, when the parents have returned to their "normal" life pattern, it may be helpful to share with them the energy pattern chart (table 5.1, on p. 59). This information can help ease the tension that so often leads to the break-up of marriages.

The Dream Child

Many people grieve for lost children without ever realizing what is causing their pain. Children born with disabilities do not match the dream babies their parents cherished during pregnancy. Yet these children are alive and must be cared for and loved. It is difficult for even loving individuals to invest themselves emotionally with this new child, who somehow did away with the dream baby they were expecting. The dream child must be

acknowledged and grieved. Only then can they fully accept and love the new child.

Similarly, as children mature and grow into toddlers and preschoolers, parents may realize that their vicarious dreams of brilliance will not be accomplished through this child. This realization can create a painful family situation. Encourage parents to lay to rest the fictional genius and allow the child to be the way he or she was created. Remind parents that most people are average. Most children in the child's class are average. Most average people have happy, creative lives.

Parents need to love their children just as they are, or they *and* their children will suffer.

Sterility and Adoption

The most painful realization for couples may be that they cannot conceive a child. For about one-sixth of all couples today, sterility is a reality. Many decide to adopt children, and then have to wait months, perhaps years. Others try to conceive by means of modern methods of insemination. For the majority of couples, because these procedures are new, this will be another disappointment.

Couples unable to conceive experience real grief. Their pain can be so intense that it is nearly visible to those around them. In addition, they have to field unthinking comments like, "So, when are you two going to start a family?"

It is crucial that couples planning to adopt complete their grieving for the biological children they could not have. If they do not, they might convey the sense that their adopted children are second best and simply replacements for the real thing. This message may never be verbalized to the children (who may be dearly loved) but children are astute, and they may sense the truth. This truth will affect their developing self-images.

You can remind adopting parents that adoption is even part of the Bible. Moses (Ex 2:1-10) was adopted, as was Jesus himself, by Joseph (Mt 1:20-25). It can be comforting to know that adoption is part of a long tradition.

Abuse and Neglect

There are some deaths that are very difficult. Especially painful is the situation wherein some neglect or abuse is suspected in the child's death. Nearly everyone feels great distress at the thought of abuse, but it is reality. You may be asked to respond with non-judgmental compassion to the adults involved. Now is a good time to think about this possibility. Would you be able to support and guide these people through what they must face? Or would your own anger at the situation increase their pain? As difficult as it seems, someone must care for these people (and not everyone can). If you know you are not the right person for the task, you can state that fact and ask that someone else reach out to that family.

RITUALIZING AT THE TIME OF DEATH

Traditional, familiar ritual can be calming when a baby is near death. It can emphasize the continuity of life and death and the continuity of the community.

Baptism

If the parents of the dying child are members of a church with a sacramental religious tradition, ask them if they want the baby baptized. In a hospital, many situations will cause this question to arise.

You might be asked to arrange for the baptism of a child in NICU (Neonatal Intensive Care Unit). The medical personnel will be helpful with this, and they have the supplies needed. If there are chaplains at the hospital, they are familiar with performing baptisms. The parents might want a priest or minister from their own community to come to the hospital if there is time, however, if neither of these resources is available, you can perform the baptism yourself.

Ask the nurses for a bottle of sterile water and a piece of cotton or gauze. If possible, have the baby's family attend the baptism. You might also invite the NICU personnel who are caring for the child. Try to create a little ceremony, as this can be comforting to the parents. Ask them to pray for their baby if they want to do so. (Listening to their prayers can give you insights into what is worrying them.) Then wet the cotton with the sterile water and place it on the child's forehead, saying, "(Child's name), I baptize you in the name of the Father, and of the Son, and of the Holy Spirit." This is the only necessary formula. You will likely want to add some statement of welcome to the Christian community.

It is a special experience to reach into an incubator and baptize a child who is not much larger than your own hand. You may be touched as never before, and many chaplains find that they are moved to tears. If this is so, the tears should not be anything to hide, for they will be a sign to the parents that their child is special to you and that you care deeply. Your tears are also a sign that God, too, is sad about their child's illness.

You may be called to the bedside of a woman in labor because it is feared that her child will be stillborn. Ask if there is a hospital chaplain who can go into the delivery room with the parents and baptize the child as soon as its head emerges. Many hospitals will welcome this intervention as it is a helpful support for the parents. If no official chaplain is available, you can ask to be permitted to perform this function.

When a child is stillborn, it is often difficult to know the exact moment of death.

I (D.R.W.) was in the delivery room in one such case, and when the baby appeared, her color was navy blue. She was very tiny, and there was no sign of life. The pediatric team was not in the room because it was expected that this baby would be born dead.

The nurse laid the baby on a table, and all the medical team went back to caring for the mother. I was standing beside the baby, praying, and I baptized her conditionally, just in case. (I have learned from experience to be careful not to assume the baby is dead.)

Just as I finished saying the baptismal formula, one little blue arm was thrown up in the air, over the baby's head. Then a leg kicked. I alerted the physician, and within seconds the pediatric team appeared from the adjacent N.I.C.U.

That baby lived for three weeks! She brought a great deal of joy to her parents and brothers. This is why most churches have authorized conditional baptism, for cases where there is not complete certainty of death.

Keep in mind, however, that baptism is a sign of membership in the Christian family and of the child's entry into Christ's death and resurrection, and into the reign of God. This sacrament is administered when someone is in danger of death, but is not administered to a dead person. Dead babies should never be baptized.

If the baby is stillborn or dies without baptism, reassure the parents that God loves their child with abundance and will not punish the child. They also need to know that they have done all they can do to assure the well-being of their child.

Catholics may need special reassurance. In the past, the Catholic church's teaching that an unbaptized infant did not go to heaven caused distress to parents whose baby died before baptism was possible. Thus infants in danger of death were baptized immediately. (Unbaptized babies were thought to go to a place called *limbo*, a state of natural happiness. The belief in limbo developed at a time when the importance of baptism was misunderstood.)

The Catholic church continues to endorse baptizing babies in danger of death and teaches that every person is "called by God's grace to salvation"[1], whether baptized or unbaptized. Baptism is not based on a belief in limbo. Rather, the desire to associate the child with the death and resurrection of Christ and to welcome the baby into the community of faith is (and always was), the motive for baptism.

Funeral or Memorial Services

Parents' need for ritual after the death of a baby can be met with a prayer service. You can suggest a funeral service for a miscarried or stillborn child. Be sensitive to whether or not the parents desire to be present. The service can take place soon after the death or on a special anniversary.

If the baby's body is not present, the ritual is called a memorial service. The purpose is the same as that of a funeral: to acknowledge that someone has lived, been loved, and died, and to pray for the family and the soul (if this suits the faith of the parents of the departed). Most clergypersons are happy to help with the service because they realize it will help the grieving parents. During the service, reassure them that they are good parents. Your (or the clergyperson's) words could go something like this:

> We are gathered tonight to acknowledge the life of Justin Franks. He didn't live very long, but he was loved by his parents, Nick and Lois. In his short life, Justin gave them a lot of joy. He heard his mother's heartbeat and voice and felt his dad rubbing on the outside of his cozy nest, and he felt safe and loved. These two people, who never had a chance to hold Justin while he was alive, nevertheless accomplished the most important task of parenting: they taught their child about love. And now Justin is in the arms of God, who is love, and he can recognize God because he learned about love from his parents.

Whatever situation you meet, remember that your most important task is to just be there. Do not stay away because you have not confronted your own fears and other emotions. Deal with these honestly. Tell the mourners if you are at a loss for words. Weep with them if it hurts you. Your honest pain may be the best tool to facilitate their grief.

Chapter Eleven

Divorce as a Grief Experience

Again, grief is the emotional, spiritual, and physical response to the loss of someone or something in whom or in which one has been strongly invested. In the context of this definition, the divorce experience may be even more traumatic than the death of a loved one.

In divorce there are two losses. One loss is the loss of a person. It is not appropriate to assume that because two adults decide to end their marriage, they are no longer emotionally invested in one another. There are all kinds of emotional investments—some more healthy than others—and all have control over the persons involved. When a woman says to her therapist, "I don't understand why I miss him so much; I was miserable every day we were together," she is hurting not only from her loss, but also because she is puzzled by her hurt. Not knowing where the hurt comes from can be even more devastating than the expected hurt of losing a loved one. Many couples who have split move back and forth, in and out of the relationship, because they cannot deal with the confusion of love/hate. The two emotions are not antithetical; in fact, they are very close in meaning. One can only be angry with a person one cares for.

Beyond the personal loss, there is the loss of the dream in which one invested: the marriage itself. A marriage is nearly a tangible thing. When one is widowed, although one's life-state changes, the image of oneself as a married person remains intact. One's life has outlasted the image. But with divorce, the image is shattered. It is rather like seeing a precious picture crashing to the ground and shattering. A part of one's life no longer exists.

Divorced people are expected by society to let go completely, perhaps even to accept the remarriage of their spouses. They may have to allow another person (who has moved into their roles) to become parent to their children! One woman said that she seemed to have ceased to exist because the frames of reference for *her* life had been given to someone *else.* This woman was grieving for her own self-definition. (Widowed persons do not have this experience because the dead spouses and the children are still seen as belonging to their lives.)

People who end a marriage often deal with the confusion of unresolved emotions. One person in the midst of a divorce may not want the relationship to end, may in fact, feel only love for the the person who has decided to leave. It is difficult when death strips a person of the spouse, but when the spouse makes a conscious decision to leave, there is often additional soul searching and an agony of failure.

Even for those who choose to leave a marriage, the leaving is painful and there is grief. Often much grieving occurs before the actual separation. There can be a great feeling of relief when it is finally ended, but even those who feel relief (because they are no longer living in situations of constant hassle or outright war) can feel a deep melancholy and sense of failure that nothing could hold together the dream. People who have had this experience often say that they are careful before entering another intimate relationship because they do not want to experience that hurt again.

Therapists are familiar with people who do not allow themselves to become deeply, emotionally intimate with others yet proclaim a strong wish for real love. When people are wounded emotionally, even though they may profess they are just fine, they naturally build invisible shells around themselves to protect them from being hurt again. With time and enough hurts, these shells become thick and strong. The person may not even know the shell exists. While these shells serve to protect people, they also isolate individuals from deep intimacy. The protection actually becomes a barrier to happiness.

This barrier can be one of the painful side effects of those who experience divorce. They may feel glad to be finished with a thoroughly unpleasant relationship, but they still suffer from the deep wound of failure and the loss of a dream. Their self-images need to be reworked, and unless they receive special support, they may subconsciously refuse to invest deeply (and vulnerably) in future relationships.

CARING FOR THE DIVORCED

Special support may be your task. People who have undergone a divorce need sensitivity and strength because they often put on strong "I'm OK" masks and almost defy caring persons to break through to their real feelings. Society does not offer them the sympathy given to widowed people, and divorced people may judge themselves as weak if they give in to their pain.

In addition, they may not have finished with their anger over the ended relationship. If you break through their masks, that anger may land on you. In other words, if your intervention brings their pain to the surface of their consciousness, they may lash out at you. They are afraid of losing control, of not appearing "put together and cool" (the image of divorced people presented by society). Wearing a mask may be the only coping skill they know.

You need to care a great deal in order to attempt helping such persons. You now become vulnerable to their anger and denial. Before even trying, ask yourself if you can receive whatever they need to hand you without internalizing it and losing faith in yourself. Ask yourself if you really want to become involved in this situation. If you have answered "Yes" to these questions, approach the person in a positive way. Share your concerns and allow the person to respond. While denial may still be strong, you will have the satisfaction that, if at some time later this person *does* need a friend with whom real pain can be shared, you have made a standing offer.

> Philip and Debra were neighbors of mine (D.R.W.) for many years. I had always known that their marriage was stormy. Their children had come over to my house several times when their parents' fighting had become too painful to bear, so I was not surprised when Debra left one day and moved to another state. She phoned the children often, telling them that they could come to her for school vacations, but she wanted nothing more to do with Philip.
>
> Before long, we heard that Debra had remarried and was expecting a child. During the months until the divorce became final, Philip had struggled with parenting their two boys, feeling lethargy and melancholy. Suddenly, when the news came of Debra's new marriage, Philip's behavior changed radically. He put on a mask of great cheer, began dating several very young women, and within a few weeks had invited one woman to move into his house with him.
>
> I was concerned for Philip for several reasons. He was a deeply religious man. His church did not approve of his living arrangements, so he dropped away from his faith community. The woman who was living with him was much younger, and Phil began spending a great deal of time at health spas and tanning parlors. While Philip had always been a rather serious person, he would no longer stop by for the long talks we had enjoyed. Instead he always seemed to be running from one social engagement to another.
>
> One day, I saw Philip sitting on his back porch. I could see his profile, and the way he held his head told me that he was troubled. I decided that I had to approach him because I needed him to know that I cared about him and that I would try to understand him. As I walked toward him, I could see his profile

change as the mask came back onto his face. I almost gave up then, but the strength of my caring forced me to continue.

"Hi, Phil. How's it going?"

"Oh, things are OK. I just came out here to have a look at the leaves one more time before they fly away and the snow comes."

This was the kind of sensitive remark the "old Philip" would have made, so I was encouraged.

"It's been a tough summer, hasn't it, old friend?"

"Oh, I don't know. I've been having a lot of fun, and I feel younger than I have in years. I had forgotten how free life can be without kids around. I guess I'll have to get used to them when they come back next week."

"I think you look great, Philip. But then, I always liked how you looked. But I have to admit that I miss our talks and times together."

"Well, that's life, I guess. I've had to make a new life for myself, and I think I'm doing a pretty good job. Got me a sweet young thing, and she thinks I'm Superman. Debra sure never treated me this good!"

"Philip, do you love Suzanne?"

"Oh, sure... I guess so. That's not really important, you know. I can't tell you how good it feels to wake up with another person beside me again."

"I can understand that, Phil. But what about the rest of the day? Do you enjoy being together? Will the boys like her when they get back?"

"Why are you asking me all these questions? It's my life! I'm not going to hurt my kids! I don't even know if Suzanne will be here by next week. So just don't be so nosy! Why do you have to always interfere?"

At this point, my inclination was to run back to the safety of my own porch, but by Philip's angry reaction, I knew I had struck a sore spot. I didn't want to leave him bleeding.

"Philip, I'll leave in a minute. But first I want to tell you that I care about you and your children. I can only imagine how deeply divorce must hurt, and to hear that Debra is making a new life without you must compound the pain."

"It's OK. We weren't happy when she was here, you know. The divorce was for the best."

"That's true. But still, it must hurt."

At this point, I saw the real Philip look at me for the first time in many months. "Yes, you know, I try not to let it hurt, but somewhere deep inside me there is this place of tears. Sometimes I dream about Debra, just her back, walking away from me."

Then his defensive expression returned. "I don't have those dreams when Suzanne is here. Donna, this is my way of getting through things. You have to let me do it my way!"

"I'm sorry, Phil, if I make you hurt by my questions. I have no intention to ask you to change your lifestyle. In fact, we would like to get to know some of your new friends, especially Suzanne.

"But I do want you to know that I care and that if you ever want to talk to a friend who will love you, no matter what, our door is always open."

Philip thanked me and stood up to go into the house, ending the conversation.

It may seem, on the surface, that nothing was accomplished by my conversation with Philip—perhaps that he was even alienated from me. It seemed that way to me, too, for several weeks. I had even come to the point of scolding myself for ever opening my mouth that day. But then, one cold January afternoon, I answered a knock on my back door to find Philip.

"Hi, Donna. I need a friend."

Our conversation that afternoon did not mean an end to my friend's confusion or pain, but it was a beginning on the journey back. He had chosen his own time, and all I had done was to let him know he had the freedom to come and talk when and if he wanted to do so.

Other Broken Relationships

Many people never legally marry but become emotionally invested in another person. This may be a friendship or a sexually intimate relationship. The important factor is that the person has learned to trust another enough to become vulnerable. If such a relationship ends, the agony will be much like divorce. One added complication is that they may have even less support than the divorcing person. Most people may not understand how deep the relationship was. (Still other people have been hurt, sometimes quite early in life, by people who let them down. They have experienced a kind of emotional divorce.)

The person who experiences an end to a relationship may be surprised at the intensity of the pain, may try to sidestep the grieving process, and may wish to simply get on with life. If you can help them to understand how deeply they were invested in the ended relationship, they may then be able to give themselves space to grieve and to feel more comfortable with their own normal emotions. Usually knowing that another person understands and validates their pain is enough to enable them to move through it.

CHILDREN OF DIVORCE

Many children today experience the profound grief of divorce. The divorce could be parents, an older sibling, or grandparents.

For some, because one parent may completely disappear, divorce is death. For others, the continuing support of both parents leadsthem directly toward healthy new definitions of the parameters of their lives.

In many cases, it is better for children if parents separate and bring them up in two happy homes rather than in one miserable home. There are two concerns when children are involved: first, to understand how family separation affects them; second, to learn how to support both the children and the parents through the pain. Even when divorce is the best option, it is not a simple procedure. To assume there will be no trauma for the children is to "play ostrich."

Remember that children are not adults. They do not perceive or care or think or feel in the same ways as adults. But their perceptions, cares, thoughts, and feelings are just as acute— only different. When you look for reactions from children, don't look for the reactions you would expect from an adult. If the children do not react to the divorce the way adults normally respond, don't assume all is fine with the children. A child may still appear to be playing normally with friends and yet be deeply troubled inside. Attempt to attune yourself to a child's ways of thinking and reacting. Try to enter the world of an adolescent or toddler; then you can offer them meaningful support.

Children's Feelings

Most adults want children to be happy. Sometimes adults even consider themselves failures if all the children around them are not smiling and having a good time. But children need as much freedom as adults to be sad or confused or angry. Think back to your childhood. Were you happy all the time? Probably not. Children are happy and unhappy about the same amount of time as adults.

There are many emotional states between "all happy" and "completely unhappy." There are reflective times, peaceful times, and many other stages of feeling. This is true for children as well as adults. When you are trying to support a child, let the child show or tell his or her feelings. You can say, "Carrie, it's a long time since I was a little person, and sometimes I forget how that feels. But I want to support you with what is happening in your life right now. I know that you are having feelings and thoughts about your parents' divorce. I hope you will tell me how it is for you, and how I can help. I can't make the divorce go away, but I think it will make things easier if you know that you have a friend who understands just how you feel."

Children's Opposition to Divorce

How do children experience their parents' marriages and its dissolution? Why do so many children oppose the ending of marriages that have been obvious disasters for years? Why do they wish that hostile parents would reunite? Parents sometimes ask, "Why can't my children accept the obvious and let us get on with giving them a better life?"

A child living in its own family perceives the family life as normal, whatever it is. Children from the most dysfunctional environment usually think that their family is normal. The unhappy rhythm in that atmosphere is the normal rhythm of the child's life. The child, as it grows into adolescence, is highly unlikely to grow out of this perception. That is why so many people repeat their parents' relationship errors. They are looking for what what they have come to perceive as normal, but what is in fact, dysfunctional.

That "normalcy" is security, the *terra firma,* of the child's life. Around this family and lifestyle, the developing child builds a self-definition. If there are fights and bitterness, or even abuse and addiction, that is the reality on which life is based. Children do not want to shake that reality.

Have you ever been in an earthquake? It happens with complete suddenness. The building and furniture, the windows and trees, and even the floor and the ground behave in ways completely contrary to what you have learned about nature.

This is not a hurricane or blizzard, a huge wave of water, or anything else you have been conditioned to fear. This is the earth, which you have come to trust as firm, acting in a completely unnatural and threatening manner, and you have no coping skills with which to deal with it.

Now imagine that you are a child and your *terra firma*, (the environment and emotional climate upon which your self-definition is based) suddenly falls apart. The only parents you have tell you they are no longer going to live together. You suddenly experience that earthquake. You cannot cope. You cannot imagine why the earth should move this way. And even once things settle down, you are still terrified by each aftershock of the separation and divorce.

Remember that the unhappy home situation seemed normal to the child. Therefore, the child cannot understand what the parents are seeking in changing the situation. "So it wasn't very good at home. So what? I'm not sure there is anything better. Why can't my parents just accept the reality of what we had and make the best of it, the way I did? At least we knew what we had." Many children often don't even realize that the marriage was falling apart because to them it appeared normal. When it is suddenly over, they are deprived of the gradual, growing awareness that things were drawing to an end. Instead children can be taken by surprise, just like the earthquake victim.

Children have an enormous need to be loved by their parents. Even if the parents are not very good at satisfying this need, children will hang around and pick up whatever crumbs land near them. The nature of the love a person receives as a child will often become the adult's definition of love, and the kind of love the adult seeks. Tragically, children learn easily that life is limited and that their own potential to be loved is flawed. They learn too quickly to accept what they get and no more. This is sometimes called coping, but it can violate the human spirit and lead to all sorts of emotional problems.

Separation

When a parent leaves, children often judge themselves unworthy of that parent's continued love. They do not see that the *parent* may have a big problem; they see it as something within themselves: their "flawed" nature (which means that they have contributed to daddy's or mommy's leaving). Divorce is as much a separation of children from the parents as it is a separation of the parents. But the adults control the situation; they make the decisions, shake the ground under the children and assume that the children should understand and accept the inevitable. To make matters worse, the child may indeed have left to live with one parent, and the other parent may strongly oppose the separation and play on the child's feelings of guilt.

The most cruel game of all those played by divorcing couples is that of dragging children through a succession of social service agencies and courts, deciding and re-deciding which parents will maintain custody. One little girl said, after her parents' seven-year custody battle, "I feel like a rubber ball." Her older sister said she felt more like an elastic band. Both of these analogies are completely dehumanizing.

Children grieve for the loss of everything familiar and stable as well as the absence (at least part-time) of one parent. Some parents say, "When I first left, I just stayed away for six weeks. I couldn't stand to go there and not stay with Billy and Ruth. I called them every weekend. But it was six weeks before I could go and spend some time with them. I hope they understand what I went through. I intend to make it up to them." If a house is destroyed in the middle of winter, it is not helpful if someone provides a shelter six weeks later and says she or he "will make it up." A homeless person might have died in the snow three weeks ago.

CARING FOR CHILDREN OF DIVORCE

The first rule for helping children going through separation and divorce is: Be there *now*. Do not assume that children have perceived their parents' relationships as disastrous. Do not assume that children see divorce as having only to do with the parents' relationship. Do not assume that, just because some of the children's friends have gone through divorce, these particular children will know how to cope. A person may have survived an earthquake and look safe and composed while inside feel terrified and confused.

You cannot control an earthquake or a divorce. But you can help children feel loved and respected, and promise that if there are any further aftershocks, you will be there for support. Encourage the parents to include their children in at least some of their arrangements so the children develop some minimal control and sense of stability. Emphasize to parents the importance of not confusing children with malicious custody battles, kidnappings, and game-playing. You can explain the dynamics of grieving to the children, and it may help them understand why their parents may be accepting the change already while they themselves are still reeling in shock. Also try to explain to the parents why the children don't understand how impossible it would be to return to the marriage. Ask the parents to be patient.

Children are resilient. Given time, most will begin to redefine the normal parameters of their lives. If things really are better at home after the divorce, they will come to see the wisdom of their parents' decision. They will place the trauma of the disaster in perspective with all other life experiences. But to accomplish these tasks they need the support, affirmation, and patience of the adults around them.

Chapter Twelve

Suicide

Suicide is a difficult topic to examine because of the intensity of the emotions surrounding the experience. Grieving over a successful suicide carries such a large mixture of anger, guilt, and denial that you as a caregiver may be overpowered and frightened away from personal contact.

It is important to study this experience for two reasons: first, suicide is striking more and more families, and the likelihood of your being asked to help in such a situation is increasing; second, the suicide statistics are directly impacted by the portion of the population with some incomplete, repressed, or maladaptive grieving in its personal psyche.

THE DEPRESSION/SUICIDE CONNECTION

Understanding some of the dynamics of depression will help in understanding the suicidal person and the person's family. The following brief description will not make you a professional psychological diagnostician, but will increase your insight into the interpersonal relations of families affected by suicide.(Much of the information about the feelings and the motivations of suicidal individuals is derived from people who try unsuccessfully to take their lives and from depressed patients who are suicidal.)

Hopelessness

People contemplating suicide usually feel hopeless. They believe that there are no answers to the pain and problems of their lives except death. (Yet many feel elated once they have made the decision and formulated the plan for suicide.)

The hopeless feeling can come from various sources. In 1929 many people had invested themselves and their self-images deeply into their financial success. When the stock market crashed, they lost their investment and could not face life with what they perceived as intolerable emptiness. This emptiness is similar to the lover who commits suicide because the beloved is unattainable. In both experiences, the individuals cannot face the perceived emptiness and the mourning tasks of such losses. In this way they are unhealthy, addicted to the objects of their infatuation.

Much more commonly, however, feelings of hopelessness and desolation are symptoms of clinical depression, a medical and psychological condition which afflicts as many as one in fifteen people at some stage of life. If severe enough, depression has a high incidence of suicidal ideation and attempts.

Clinical Depression

Clinical depression can come from many sources. Sometimes it is inherited and may strike a person suddenly or creep up over years. Any person who lives in an abusive situation or other environment that creates significant repressed anger may eventually develop severe depression.

Professional caregivers individually diagnose possible reasons for depression. Those who are not professional psychological caregivers must understand that in cases of clinical depression, many times people cannot heal themselves and are unable to respond to talking therapy or psychotherapy, because the clinically depressed person's brain has changed in its functioning, sending messages to the body to secrete depressing chemicals (which may lead the person to suicidal thoughts). As long as the body's chemistry flows in this manner, the person cannot, no matter how hard he or she tries, respond to good wishes and care. The body itself is fighting any efforts toward healing. Medical professionals do not know exactly how this works. The prevailing theory is that the chemicals in the brain that act as the media for thought messages become abnormal. Psychiatrists do know which medications are usually helpful to treat clinical depression.

Negative Perceptions

Because the perceptions of a clinically depressed person and a healthy person will often differ, functioning in the family and workplace can cause much tension. The depressed person has a negative self-image and thus perceives most environmental or interpersonal relationships as negative. Typically a depressed teen-ager will spend most free time in her room, retreating from a world that seems threatening and retreating from both family and teachers because they appear to be the enemy. A depressed senior citizen may seem paranoid, secret himself in his room, and refuse all offers of love or help, thinking that those who want to help are actually there to harm him.

These negative perceptions can make it difficult to persuade a depressed person to seek help. Often they have so alienated the people around them because of this negative attitude, those people withdraw and seek more pleasant company. Other times, caring people persistently urge the depressed person to get professional help, but since part of depression is the perception that everyone is the enemy, the last thing the depressed person will do is take advice. If the depression involves a chemical imbalance, the person needs medical help or recovery is impossible.

CARING FOR THE DEPRESSED
AND SUICIDAL PERSON

Depressed people may not be able to experience any joy or hope. They cannot control their own thought processes, cannot switch from negative thoughts and try to "cheer up." If you tell someone who is depressed to do so, you may only alienate the person and jeopardize your chances of reaching out to that person in any way.

With clinical depression, you as caregiver must help the depressed person's family and friends to understand the urgency of finding medical care for this person, even if it means the use of gentle force. Because ill people have perceptions which are abnormally negative, they are incapable of making decisions about their own care. And if the person hints at suicide, care is absolutely necessary, even if the person must be forced. We cannot emphasize this too strongly; too many families end up in emergency rooms or morgues, claiming their loved one's body because they let things slide, hoping a depressed person would improve or "snap out of it."

As a caregiver, you likely will come in contact with persons who have suicidal thoughts. Clues to these thoughts may be given indirectly. Depressed people may give away prized possessions, withdraw from relationships, and make comments about life not being important or of value. If you hear a depressed person say "I wish I were dead," you must take the person seriously! It will not help to give them reasons for living; just listen with care, love, and understanding.

If people talk about committing suicide, inform them that you are obligated to tell their family or someone who loves them. Your immediate responsibility is to get them to go for professional help. If after the first mention of suicide, they tell you they weren't serious, you must still act on what they told you earlier. If they have thought and talked about it once, they may again, and the next time they may carry out the act. Inform the person to whom you are responsible as caregiver. They can give you assistance and support. You should never try to deal with a suicidal person by yourself.

It is your responsibility to care, help, and intervene. But you cannot be held responsible for the suicidal person who makes a decision to end life and succeeds in doing so. If this happens you will likely experience strong feelings and will need to deal with them. (See chapter six.) You also may need assistance from another caring person.

CARING FOR THE SURVIVORS

More often each year, ministers receive calls to help a family whose member committed suicide. Caregivers express to us that upon entering the home, the feeling level is so intense that it almost hits them physically as they come in the door. They expected grief, but what was present was overwhelming confusion, denial, and anger.

Remember that the negative atmosphere of a home probably builds, sometimes for years,when a depressed person is present. The family often becomes severely dysfunctional as each member tries to find a way to behave that will not arouse the depressed person's negative perceptions. Honest communication may cease. Perhaps anger boils barely below the surface. Healthy family members can be confused and hurt, feeling unloved by the depressed person, not understanding how to re-open communication lines. If the depressed person is a child, the parents may feel like failures; if the depressed person is an adult, the spouse or children may adopt a guilty attitude and learn to lie when the depressed member acts in socially unacceptable ways.

When the depressed person commits suicide, all the emotions and dysfunctional behavior of the family become stronger. A wall may be put up to protect the family from what it perceives as the judgment of others. For the human psyche, the pain at this time is one of the most intense possible. Enter this situation with great patience because your patience may be greatly tried.

One way to gain strength is to pray. Ask God to help you become centered before entering the distressed environment. Also ask yourself, "Why am I going here? What are my personal motivations?" Answering honestly will help you determine if you are really the best person to go or whether your motivations involve curiosity or judgment. You must understand yourself, or you may lose sight of your mission in such a high-tension atmosphere.

Once you are aware of your motivations, if you are Christian, ask yourself how Jesus might approach this family. What was his usual attitude toward broken people? We experience Jesus as compassionate and empathetic, and as someone who tried to discover what people needed and who accepted people just as they were.Therefore, maintain an open mind and be prepared to accept whatever "space" these people are in. Assure them that there are no right or wrong reactions to this pain.

One common reaction of families is denial. But rather than denying the death itself, they deny that the death occurred by the person's own hand. Thus they speak of "the accident" or "John's illness." This denial may be part of the dysfunctional lying they learned to do while living with the depressed person. Or it may be that the situation is so new that they simply cannot bring themselves to say "that word."

Listen to them explain the cause of death to someone who doesn't know. If they tell an intricate tale—for example, describing the details of an auto accident—then you will know where they are. But if they simply admit, "Yes, Susan's death was quite sudden," or something less committal, in time they probably will be able to tell the truth. Remember that if most people have a hard time accepting death itself, they have a harder time accepting that death occurred in a "socially unacceptable" way. Until recently suicide was considered criminal behavior. For Roman Catholics it is a serious moral dilemma,but because of an increased understanding of human behavior, a sense of guilt is mitigated. For example, in *The Code of Canon Law*[1] funerals are now permitted and compassion is always extended to the family. (Caregivers should be aware that for some Catholics the notion of sin may increase their sense of stigma.)

I (D.R.W.) was asked to meet with a couple whose sixteen-year-old daughter had been brought to the emergency room of the hospital where I worked. She was dead on arrival. As I entered the head nurse's office where they were sitting, I saw a couple about sixty years old, sitting in separate chairs. The man held his head in his hands, and the woman was sitting up straight without much expression on her face. They did not acknowledge my arrival, but when I introduced myself, they both looked at me. Just then, a man about twenty-five years old burst through the door behind me. He rushed over to the woman and knelt beside her. She looked at him with no expression.

"Mother," he said. "What has happened? The hospital called me and said that Yoli had been brought in. Is she OK? Is she hurt?"

It was the father who answered. "David, Yoli has had a terrible accident. The doctor's can't help her." The mother's face still registered little expression.

"What do you mean, 'can't help her'? Did you call Dr. Torres?"

Seeing that neither of the parents was about to answer (the man had his head down and the woman seemed numb), I said, "Mr. D., your sister has died, just a few minutes before she arrived at the hospital. The paramedics tried to restart her heart, but they couldn't. When the ambulance got here, Yoli was pronounced dead."

"Did she have a heart attack? My God, how could a kid have a heart attack?"

Again, no response from the parents, so I said, "No, Yoli didn't have a heart attack. Her heart stopped because she took some drugs while she was at home."

"But why would she take drugs? Was she sick?...Oh, no....You don't mean...?"

There was a long pause. Finally, the father looked up and said, "David, we think that Yoli must have wanted to die." His last words were sobbed to his son, who was now slumped over beside his mother's chair.

I put my arms around him and said, "This is hard to hear, isn't it? I wish we never had to give this particular news to people. But unfortunately, what your father said is true. Your sister took an overdose of medication, and we think she did it on purpose."

Nobody, so far, had said the word "suicide." We did not need to; there are kinder ways to share this news.

I left the family alone for a few minutes and went to get some water for them. When I returned, things were pretty much as I had left them. David was asking the room in general, "Does anybody know why? Oh God, tell me why. We love her so much!"

"I know that you love her, David. But sometimes when a person is sad and depressed, she can't accept or enjoy the love that is there. I know that because someone I loved did the same thing. Although I asked myself if I had failed him, in the end we realized that sometimes people do not love themselves enough to accept other people's love. That was very sad to know, but at least I realized that his death wasn't my fault."

Suddenly, the mother stood up and shouted, "*Damn her!* She just had to do something that would hurt us this much. All the other things, the boys and the drugs and the stealing, those were things we could deal with. We were in control. But now she has punished us forever!" I went to her, and she collapsed in my arms.

After a few minutes, I said, "It sounds as if Yoli had been acting angrily for a while." They nodded. "Suicide (I felt they could handle this word in a clinical sense and not referring specifically to Yoli) is often an angry act people use to manipulate or punish the people who love them. You may be right, Mrs. D. But I would like you to listen to me, please, because what I am going to say might help you understand."

I sensed that I had their attention, so I continued. "Just because a teen-ager commits this angry act doesn't mean she doesn't love her family. Teen-agers can get mixed up, especially if they are depressed, and their thinking gets unclear. Kids who tried suicide but did not succeed say they had pictured the scenes after their deaths—all their loved ones weeping—and then coming back and telling their families what they had wanted to say before. In other words, they did not perceive their death as final, but as a way to manipulate their environment and the people in it. I hope you can believe that Yoli did love you but was so mixed up that she made a big mistake. Unfortunately, that mistake was final."

The family had been listening as I spoke. They took a few minutes to think, and the mother's expression began to soften and the father looked up. Finally, the son asked the usual question about what to do next. After explaining the necessary legalities and forms, I asked if they wanted to talk further before they left. Mrs. D. said, "I don't know what to tell people. What do I say to my mother or to the neighbors? And what about Yoli's friends—they are only children! How do I tell them?"

I went over and took her hand. My heart hurt for this family. "Mrs. D., it's a hard thing to do. You may want to take a few hours to think about it and talk to your husband and son. I know you are concerned about how hurt your mother will be, and I certainly understand your worry. You know her best, and you are the only one who can decide if she needs to know the whole truth right away, or if you want to tell her the details a bit at a time.

"As for the others, they will find out the truth. People always do, so it's best the hear it from you. Lies only damage trust in any relationship.

"Her friends have thought about suicide more than you can imagine. Their biggest hurt will be that Yoli is gone, not how it happened. If you feel able, I urge you to share with them that this is not the answer and that there are better alternatives. It may give some meaning to this tragedy if her friends learn something from it. That is not something you need to do today, but think about it for the future.

"You might be surprised how many of your friends and neighbors have experienced this sort of thing themselves. They will likely be more supportive than you expect. Why don't you trust them?"

Her husband said, "Emma, we'll do it together. Don't be afraid." He put his arm around her. "I think we should go home now and think about what to do next. We really thank you for your help. May we tell someone to call you if they have questions?"

I assured them that I was available, gave them my card, then walked them to their car. I felt these people would make it through their pain because they were already talking about their loss and expressing their emotions.

I planned to contact them in a couple of weeks, realizing that people in this situation have trouble reaching out for help.

Ministering to the family that has experienced a suicide is never easy. If you can be centered, be aware of the non-verbal messages, and have a non-judgmental attitude, you will be able to help. The pain takes a long time to go away, but if you model a community that accepts and loves, this tragedy will be slightly lighter to bear.

Chapter Thirteen

Funerals

There are as many way to ritualize the closure of death as there are creative minds to celebrate these rituals. This chapter is not intended to tell you of any "best" way to help mourning families effect closure. Rather, we will herein give you some thoughts and ideas. All of this is meant to convey one central theme: *Funeral rituals are meant to help, comfort, and support the grieving person. Any other benefit, such as the building of community or evangelization, is secondary. If the funeral does not minister to those who are in pain, it has failed.*

Last year, I (D.R.W.) was at a good friend's funeral. The priest spoke for about thirty minutes. He outlined a tremendously powerful theology of resurrection, illustrating each point from Scripture, telling amusing anecdotes, and generally showing the assembled people that he had given a great deal of thought to this subject.

While all this was being said, the husband of the dead woman sat in the front row, his head in his hands. When the priest finally stopped speaking and the choir began to sing, he suddenly looked up. He blinked a few times as if he was awaking from a dream.

After the funeral, I heard someone remark, "Didn't Father Tim give a wonderful talk? He really made me think!"

I thought to myself, "But that wasn't why you were here. He can make people think on Sundays or so many other times. Today, he was supposed to be making the hurting family aware that the community cares and will support them, that their wife and mother have experienced resurrection, and that the community has assembled as a sign of shared faith and love."

FUNERAL ARRANGEMENTS

There are many ways you can reach out to those who are mourning, through the funeral and through the other grief rituals of your faith community. The trip to the mortuary is often difficult. Funeral directors and morticians have been labeled as opportunistic, waiting to pounce upon mourners for financial gain. In reality, most are highly compassionate and ethical professionals happy to help mourners arrange whatever type of funeral they want. But because these arrangements are most often made when grief and numbness are acute, it is hard for grieving people to decide what they want.

It can be helpful for someone to accompany the grieving family as they choose burial sites, caskets, and other funeral arrangements. If you do this, sit down with the family at home first. Ask them about what kind of arrangements they are hoping to make. Then, when they are in the highly-charged atmosphere of the funeral home, where so many options are presented, you can gently remind them of their preferences. They are free to change their minds, but you can help them to feel as if the choices were their own, not those of the salesperson.

If you have never been to a funeral home, make an appointment to speak with a funeral director in your area. Ask what options are usually presented and why. Ask which choices are most popular with persons in your faith community. You may be surprised at how much the funeral director knows about your congregation.

Speak with your clergyperson, and ask about preferences within your denomination and community. Is there a specific mortuary and cemetery that is preferred? Does your faith group oppose embalming or cremation? Is there any preference for or against an open casket at funerals? Once you have this information, you can be much more helpful to people who are grieving.

The best time to arrange a funeral is before it is needed. People can choose their own arrangements, knowing there will be no emotional or financial burden on their families. This gives a strong sense of control to many people who are ill. But the best time is even before illness, when everyone is strong and well and expects to live a long time. One added advantage of the pre-arranged funeral is that, if the person does not die for several years, a great deal of money can be saved. The person only pays what the funeral cost at the time of arrangement.

Think about planning a seminar at your church or temple. Invite some funeral directors from the community so that people could learn about funeral arrangements and how to plan and purchase their own.

PLANNING THE SERVICE

As well as choosing burial sites and caskets, there is the actual funeral service to be planned. Within some faith groups, these services are planned according to the preference of the clergyperson and family; other denominations have set rites that must be followed. It is usually wise to involve the mourners in planning the funeral service. Sometimes clergypersons do not want to do this because the mourners do not really understand how a funeral service is structured. This is one of those circumstances in which caregivers can make some liaison between grieving family and the faith community. It is usually possible—although it may be more work—to hear the needs of the grieving family and somehow incorporate them into an acceptable service. Many people will have wonderful ideas about how to really personalize the service with words or music that will be especially helpful to their family. At the very least, the person's name should be used in the way it commonly was used in life. A woman who was named "Kate" for 67 years should not suddenly become "Kathleen" at her funeral. The funeral is meant to remember the person's life and should reflect something about who the person really was.

DIFFERING NEEDS OF MOURNERS

Funeral rites can be a source of division among people. Sometimes you will be working with a dying person who states that no funeral is to be held. Their family may be hurt by this, feeling a need for a ceremony of closure to the person's life. You feel caught in the middle, wanting to keep the wishes of the dying person but also understanding the needs of the family. Or one member of the family may say, "John really wanted to be cremated. I think we should do that." Another person is violently opposed to cremation, and the family begins to feud. There are no easy answers to these concerns. In the end, decisions have to be made and lived with, and the best thing you can do is to facilitate dialogue between family members so that they arrive at a plan with which they all can live.

Two sisters in late middle age sat in my (D.R.W.'s) office one cold day in January. Their brother had died, and they had attended his funeral in another city. Now they were angry with each other and had come to me to ask me to help them understand why.

"We are really a close family," said Margaret, who was as tiny as her sister was huge. "We are all very different, but in the end, we hold the same values. That's why I was shocked by what our sister-in-law did at Bob's funeral."

"I don't know why you should be shocked," puffed Winnie. "We knew she made him join that other religion, and it seemed to make him happy. So why should you expect them to change when it came time for the funeral?"

"Well, I knew it wouldn't be quite the same. But my goodness, it wasn't even really a funeral! There was no body—something about not grieving for the earthly remains—and we stood out in this park, and they had balloons for everyone, and there was no minister at all!"

Winnie explained. "Our brother was an artist. They didn't really go to a church, but they would meet with friends on Sunday evenings and worship what they called the 'parent creator.' Most of their friends were artists and into creativity and such.

"Well, for the funeral, they brought a whole bunch of Bob's work out into the park, and it was all leaning against trees and shrubs. Then each friend stood up and spoke or read something that made them think of Bob. One woman sang a song she wrote just for him. Then they would say, 'Good-bye, Bob,' and let their balloon go.

"I thought it was really pretty, and I wanted to speak too. But Margaret wouldn't do it, and now she wants to find a priest who will have a 'proper' funeral for Bob."

"I don't think we should do that. Bob had the kind of funeral he wanted. We should leave things alone."

"The kind of funeral he wanted was not a funeral at all!" Margaret straightened up on the chair so her tiny feet dangled inches from the floor. "We all know he was misled into leaving the church, and this is just an example of that. I think he should have a proper, Christian service."

I listened to both sisters. Obviously they both cared a great deal about their family. Margaret had been correct in saying that they were very different in more ways than looks. She was the kind of person who is attached to tradition and sees anyone who moved away from it as "misled." Winnie, on the other hand, was more like her offhand artist brother and, even within the traditional church structure, she was usually to be found among those who moved for change and modern worship practice.

But there was an even deeper difference. After some questions, I ascertained that Winnie's personal image of God was one of acceptance, that God rarely dictated specific human behaviors but lovingly supported people as they made their way through life. On the other hand, Margaret's God was a maker of rules, a judge and punisher. She was sincerely worried about the state of her brother's soul if he were not properly "prayed into heaven."

Once both sisters had articulated their God images to each other, Winnie could understand Margaret's concern. She realized that her sister wasn't just being hard on their brother or his wife but was really trying to help.

Winnie did not try to persuade Margaret that God would not judge Bob harshly if he had no "proper" funeral. Instead, she helped her to plan a memorial service, which was held in the chapel of their church and was led along traditional lines by their minister. This was a healing time for both sisters. They even invited Bob's widow, explaining that they felt the need for a memorial service in the city where Bob had grown up. She came, bringing Bob's self-portrait, which was displayed in the church.

This is an example of a caregiver helping a family to understand each other's preferences. Usually there is a reason for these preferences, but often nobody has articulated it. Once the family members understand *why* each other has needs, they can usually deicde upon something everyone can accept.

AFTER THE FUNERAL

Often after all the excitement and support of the funeral time is over, people are left with a period of deep emptiness. This emptiness is made worse because for many the numbness of early grief is wearing off. Now reality must be faced, but all the family and friends have returned to their own lives and seem busy and involved again.

Jewish Customs

To deal with this time, Jewish tradition provides a healthy and supportive way that both marks them as mourners and provides ritual mourning. It begins with a condolence meal at the family home prepared by caring friends. (First on the menu are boiled eggs that grow harder with time, just as the pain of grief grows harder.) For a period of three to seven days, the family will be at home "sitting *shiva*" and people call to express condolences.

During this time, *minyan* services are held at the temple to remember the deceased. For thirty days, the family wears torn clothing, marking them as mourners, and they will notnot attend social functions other than baby namings, *Bar* and *Bat Mitzvahs*, and weddings. This period of official mourning is called *sheloshim* meaning "thirty." After a year, the gravestone is placed as a permanent memorial.

> Our experience is that, when taken seriously, these Jewish mourning customs "work" in the sense that they do require us to confront the reality of death, reintegrate our lives in a new way, and emerge on the other side of the process of grieving as a more loving and compassionate human being.[1]

This should be the ideal in any grieving rite.

Additional Customs

Christians also practice many helpful rituals after the funeral. Some churches have groups of people whose special ministry is in preparing a reception for mourners. Often family and close friends will take turns staying for several days in the house of the principal mourners so that they are not alone. The Roman Catholic practice of celebrating memorial Masses and sending prayer cards to the bereaved can be comforting. Many people also have a special service a year after the death.

Many cultures have developed practices that answer the need to ritualize grief.

> I (D.R.W.) recently heard a man remark that he found the custom of Mexican Americans spending weekend afternoons sitting at the graveside of dead relatives to be a rather gruesome ordeal. I replied that I live right beside a predominantly Mexican cemetery, and I am often touched to look out and see families gathered together and sitting beside an immaculately tended grave. They are sharing memories, touching each other's pain, and reassuring themselves that they are showing respect for the person who died. In its best form, this is a wonderful way to help each other through a time of intense pain.

If you are asked to help a family that has persons from another faith group or culture, ask about mourning customs and try to understand why they developed. You can use these customs to help you as you respond to the family's needs.

PRACTICAL GUIDANCE

Many faith communities are developing resources to help their members with funeral and mourning arrangements. An especially good booklet has been developed by Rabbi Jonathan M. Brown of Temple Israel in Long Beach, California. Available to all temple members, it answers just about any question they could ask. It explains the availability of the rabbinical staff in addition to other temple societies that help with grieving. (For information on ordering, see Appendix B.) Many mortuaries and hospitals also offer helpful literature, not only about their services but about grief and funeral planning.

To share this time of acute pain with a family is a touching, sacred moment, from which you will emerge a wiser, more sensitive human being. To be trusted as a caregiver, to be accepted as an "insider," is a beautiful gift requiring sensitivity and joy in God's call to minister to the pain and hopes of the grieving.

Conclusion

The natural world around us changes constantly. People experience the newness of spring's green leaves and then see them die and fall to the ground in autumn. Many people resist change because there is comfort and security in the familiar and because change involves loss.

> I (D.R.W.) was at a public event recently, and just in front of me was a couple who elicited from me a feeling of sadness. They looked to be in their mid-sixties. He had a bright shirt and tight jeans, and around his neck he wore several heavy gold chains. The woman wore a short purple mini-skirt and an off-the-shoulder blouse. Both of them had back-combed blonde hair and deep tans.
>
> Why did I feel so sad about this couple? To me, their appearance said they had bought into the youth culture of society and were feeling insecure about the natural aging process of their bodies. Something within these two people was screaming out against the passage of time, and that scream was reflected in their appearance.

For each life transition a person makes, there is a need to grieve. Obviously, the grief process for major transitions will be deeper and longer, but everyone needs to be aware that life's changes involve transition, loss, and grieving. Most people deal with major grief crises such as divorce or death in much the same

181

way they dealt with past, less traumatic events. Grief experiences can be like bricks: they build up, one upon the other, until finally a strong wall is created.

A woman from Belfast spoke to me (D.R.W.) of a childhood experience. The Catholic and public schools were beside each other, but a high brick wall separated the boys' play areas. At recess, boys from both schools would lob stones and sticks over the wall at each other. This is typical of the communication that brick walls foster.

The book and the accompanying teaching program aim to cut doors in walls and eventually break them down completely. We hope that, by reading what we've shared, some of your walls have crumbled. If this is so, please share your new insights with others.

Believe in yourself, and in God's power within you.
With the help of our loving God,
the hearts of many will become more whole.

Appendix A

JEWISH RITUALS AT THE TIME OF DEATH

The *Mi Shebeirach* can bring great comfort. It begins, "May he who blessed our ancestors, Abraham, Isaac, Jacob, Sarah, Rebecca, Rachel, and Leah, bless and heal _____."

For those nearing death, *Shinui Hashan*, the ceremonial changing of the name is sometimes significant. Jewish people believe that a person's name greatly influences that individual's life. The creation story illustrates this: the human person, who is to be master over all other creatures, names them. Through the naming it is recognized that no existing creature can be a helpmate for the person into whom God breathed life.

> *So from the soil Yahweh fashioned all the wild animals and all the birds of heaven. These he brought to the man to see what he would call them; each one was to bear the name the man would give it. The man gave names to all the cattle, all the birds of heaven and all the wild animals. But no helper suitable for the man was found for him (Gen 2:19-20).*

Because of the belief in the importance of the person's name (which supports the person's identity), when the ceremony changes the name to a new, life-bearing or life-nurturing name, it can bring great emotional and spiritual comfort and support to the ill person. This ritual also forms a healthy psychological bridge between the past, present, and future realities of the sick person's life.

As the person is dying, those present stand, look in to the person's face, and recite:

> *The Lord reigns, the Lord has reigned,*
> *and the Lord will reign for ever and ever.*
> *Blessed be his name, whose glorious kingdom*
> *is forever and ever. (three times)*
> *The Lord, He is God. (seven times)*
> *Hear, O Israel, the Lord our God,*
> *the Lord is ONE. (seven times)*

If the soul does not depart the words, "The Lord is ONE" are to be recited over and over so that the soul will be escorted from this world. At the moment of death, all mourners are expected to rend some part of their garments. For one month this rent garment will signify mourning. Within Judaism the way this service is conducted varies, but the basic concepts remain the same.

Appendix B

FUNERAL BOOKLET

Rabbi Brown developed a booklet for his congregation entitled, *A Time to Mourn: A Guide to Funeral Practices and Mourning Ritual.* It could serve as a model for any faith community. For further information write (or phone):

Shirley Loeb
Temple Israel
3538 East Third Street
Long Beach, CA 90803-1038
(213) 434-0996

Notes

Foreword
[1] Jure Kristo, "The Interpretation of Religious Experience," *The Journal of Religion* (January 1982), 21.

Introduction
[1] The accompanying *Facilitator's Manual* is scheduled for printing in 1991.
[2] Chaim Potok, *My Name is Asher Lev,* (New York: Knopf, 1972), 156.
[3] Iris Bolton, "My Son... My Son,"date and place of publication unknown.
[4] Elizabeth Kubler-Ross, *Death the Final Stage of Growth* (Englewood Cliffs, New Jersey: Prentice-Hall, 1974), x.
[5] Alla Bozarth-Campbell, *Life is Goodbye, Life is Hello* (Minneapolis: Compcare Publishers, 1982), 176.

Chapter One
[1] André Rochais, *Personality and Human Relations* (France: unpublished Program for Personal Growth, 1984).
[2] Ibid.
[3] Ibid.
[4] Rev. Lawrence Shelton, *Ministry Reflection and Assessment: Permanent Diaconate Program* (Los Angeles: Archdiocese of Los Angeles, 1989), 2.

Chapter Two
[1] Michael Appleton, "Teaching Medical Students About Death and Dying," *The American Journal of Hospice Care* (March-April 1985), 24, 26.

Chapter Seven
[1] Christopher Jay Johnson, Ph.D, and Marsha G. McGee, Ph.D ed., *Encounters With Eternity: Religious Views of Death and Life After Death* (New York: Philosophical Library, 1986), 93.

Chapter Ten
[1] Austin Flannery, ed., The Dogmatic Consitution on the Church," *Vatican Council II: The Conciliar and Post Conciliar Documents* (Northport, New York: Costello, 1975), 365.

Chapter Twelve
[1]James A. Coriden, Thomas J. Green, Donald E. Heintschel, eds., *The Code of Canon Law: Text and Commentary* (Mahwah, New Jersy: Paulist Press, 1985), 839-840.

Chapter Thirteen
[1] Rabbi Jonathan M. Brown, *A Time to Mourn: A Guide to Funeral Practices and Mourning Ritual* (Long Beach, California: Temple Israel), 15-16.

Further Reading

Bridges, William. *Making Sense of Life's Transitions: Strategies for Coping with the Difficult, Painful and Confusing Times in Your Life*. Reading, Mass.: Addison-Wesley Publishing Company, 1980.

Coleman, William L. *What Children Need to Know When Parents Get Divorced*. Minneapolis, Minn.: Bethany House Publishers, 1983.

Colgrove, Melbe; Harold H. Bloomfield; Peter McWilliams. *How to Survive the Loss of a Love: A Different Kind Of Guide To Overcoming All Your Emotional Hurts*. New York: Bantam Books, 1976.

Grollman, Earl A., ed. *Concerning Death: A Practical Guide for the Living*. Boston: Beacon Press, 1974.

Knowles, Donald W., and Nancy Reeves. *But Won't Granny Need Her Socks? Dealing Effectively with Children's Concerns About Death and Dying*. Dubuque: Kendall/Hunt Publishing Company, 1983.

Kopp, Ruth, and Stephen Sorenson. *When Someone You Love Is Dying*. Grand Rapids, Mich.: Ministry Resources Library, Zondervan Publishing House, 1980.

Kushner, Harold S. *When Bad Things Happen to Good People.* New York: Schocken Books, 1981.

Manning, Doug. *Don't Take My Grief Away: What To Do When You Lose a Loved One.* San Francisco: Harper and Row, 1979.

Rupp, Joyce, O.S.M. *Praying Our Goodbyes.* Notre Dame: Ave Maria Press, 1988.

Staudacher, Carol. *Beyond Grief: A Guide for Recovering from the Death of a Loved One.* Oakland, Calif.: New Harbinger Publications, 1987.

Vanauken, Sheldon. *A Severe Mercy.* With letters by C. S. Lewis. New York: Bantam Books, 1977.

Weirsbe, Warren S. *Why Us? When Bad Things Happen to God's People.* Old Tappan, New Jersey: Fleming H. Revell Company, 1984.

Index

192

(Caring for)
parents of dying child, 123-126, 134-140
survivors of suicide,163-169
Chaplain
See Clergyperson
Clergyperson (chaplain, minister), 19, 32, 66, 80, 100, 134, 143, 145-146, 173, 174
Communication, 70, 81-83
Control, 23-24, 31, 47, 100, 130, 149, 173
abusing, 23
aging and, 23, 32
children and, 23
illness and, 24, 27, 30, 32
independence and, 24-25, 48

D

Death
as stage of life, 31
euphemisms for, 21, 38, 41, 46, 114
image of, 97-99
of a sibling, 119
of a spouse, 37, 40
Denial, 19, 41-43
before death, 43
danger of, 45
learning, 18-19
moving through, 45-46
society and, 18, 97
suicide and, 165

usefulness of, 45
Depression, 99, 159-163
as a phase of grief, 54-55
clinical, 160-161
hopelessness and, 160
suicide and, 159-161
Despair, 41, 99
Disabilities
children with, 140-42
Divorce, 18, 35, 40, 60, 147-158
children and, 18, 61, 63, 153-158
remarriage and, 148
Doctor
See Physician
Drawing
See Art, use of

E

Education (school, university)
nurses and physicians, 21, 28
Emotional illness
and children, 124
Emotions (feelings)
acknowledgement of, 74-75, 83-85, 99, 106, 110, 134
ambivalent feelings, 38
denial of, 72
impairment of, 37
in the Bible, 71-72
investment of, 34, 36, 41, 140, 147, 152-153
Empathy, 85-86
Eye contact, 77-78

F

Facilitator's Manual, 3
Fear, 2, 21, 28, 99
Feelings
See Emotions
Forgiveness, 96, 100-101
Funeral, 17, 20, 24, 46,
   171-179
   burial, 16, 18, 172, 174
   differing customs after,
      177-178
   for baby, 145-146
   mortuary, 172-173, 179
   needs of mourners, 174-
   177
   planning, 109, 172-177,
   179
   purpose of, 171
   viewing body, 46
   wake, 18
Funeral booklet
See Appendix B

G

God, 1-3, 7-11, 13, 32, 48,
   53, 56, 69, 85-86, 88
   bargaining with, 50-51, 54
   image of, 48, 97-98, 107-
   108, 134-137
   listening to, 107
Grief
   acceptance phase, 40
   acute phase, 40
   anniversary, 65
   being "stuck" in, 39, 66

definition of, 35
disorientation and, 42
duration of, 36, 65
dynamics of, 35, 38
energy used for, 59-60
phases of, 39-40, 42
physical symptoms, 36, 58
preparatory, 38-39
symptoms of, 58
transition phase, 40
Grief counselor, 20, 36, 47,
   50
Grief cycle, 58
Grief work, 36, 66
Grieving implications of
   loss, 63
Guilt, 36, 99, 123

H

Hospice, 21, 100
Hospital, 16-17, 28, 100, 179
   grief support program in,
   66
Identifying your gifts
   See Ministry, discernment
   of
Inner self, 13-14
Islamic ritual
   See Ritual, religious

J

Jesus, 2, 4, 8-9, 48, 51, 55,
   70-71, 142
Jewish ritual
   See Ritual, religious
Journey, 6, 39, 54

COUNSELING RESOURCES

CALL TO COMFORT:
A Counseling Manual for Every Christian
by Tom Yarbrough
Paperbound $7.95, 131 pages, 5½" x 8½", ISBN 0-89390-119-9
By combining biblical principles, personal anecdotes, and psychological tools, the author shows you how to prepare for informal counseling and what 'equipment' you need. In addition, he shows you specific steps for your first counseling endeavor and provides a work manual containing extra help.

LISTENING WITH LOVE:
True Stories from Peer Counseling
Revised Edition
by Joan Sturkie
Cloth $16.95, ISBN 0-89390-151-2
Paper $9.95, ISBN 0-89390-150-4
270 pages, 6" x 9"
Teacher's Guide to Listening With Love
Paper $9.95

64 pages, 5 ½" x 8 ½", ISBN 0-89390-161-X
Listening With Love explains peer helping: a program that trains young people to help each other. Includes section on how to start and maintain such a program. These stories from the actual lives of students can be used to generate discussion of problems which are universal among young people today. Or use the *Teacher's Guide* to plan out a semester course in peer helping, with the stories from *Listening With Love* as the text.

THE PEER COUNSELOR'S POCKET BOOK
by Joan Sturkie and Valerie Gibson
Paperbound $9.95
74 pages, 4¼" x 7", ISBN 0-89390-162-8
The peer counselor's basic tool, a handy guide and reference book for pocket or purse that includes the essentials of peer counseling. Includes a section for telephone numbers and local referral agencies.

WHISPERS OF THE HEART:
A Journey Toward Befriending Yourself
by Dale R. Olen
Paperbound $8.95
180 pages, 5½" x 8½", ISBN 0-89390-100-8
Human behavior arises from fundamental core energies that are good: the energy to exist, the energy to act freely, the energy to love. Get in touch with these energies and learn to celebrate your own goodness. Your behavior will improve, as well as your sense of fulfillment and growth.

MINISTRY RESOURCES

RCIA MINISTRY
An Adventure into Mayhem and Mystery
by Bobbie Hixon
Paperbound $9.95, 120 pages, 5½ x 8½", ISBN 0-89390-156-3
If you are involved in the RCIA ministry don't miss this powerful new book. Bobbie Hixon warns that RCIA is not something you "do" to someone else. It's something that happens to you as much as to the catechumen. The author takes you deep into the process of the adult catechumenate and shows you how each step — from pre-catechumenate to mystagogia — will turn your world upside down.

MINISTRY IN A MESSY WORLD
A New Model for Effective Ministry
by Jerry Welte
Paperbound $9.95, 176 pages, 5½" x 8½", ISBN 0-89390-154-7
Are you a professional minister, member of a pastoral team, or someone involved in a caring relationship? If so, it is time for re-evaluation and re-formation of your ongoing ministry. Jerry Welte will show you that effective ministry must be in touch with the extreme desperation and hopelessness that characterizes many human lives. This book defines the mess you are up against, then offers you realistic suggestions (and lots of hope) for your ministry.

"This book...takes ministry out of the realm of fantasy and puts it squarely into reality, but without a trace of weariness and in a manner that can bring liberation."
— Charles L. Winters, Professor of Christian Ministries, Seabury-Western Theological Seminary

IN THE POTTER'S HANDS
Nine Wake Services
by Robert Eimer, O.M.I., and Sarah O'Malley, O.S.B.
Paperbound $6.95, 71 pages, 5½" x 8½",ISBN 0-89390-132-6
Your wake services must be flexible, interchangeable, and personal if you want to comfort bereaved family members. Choose the most appropriate service by Scripture selection, symbol, theme, or season.

"This is a practical, functional, and creative resource that should be in the hands of all who work on bereavement teams. Mortuaries should include them as aids for services."
— Sister Anthony Poerio, I.B.V.M.,
Director, Office of Worship, Diocese of Phoenix

ORDER FORM --
Order from your local religious bookstore, or mail this form to:

Qty	Title	Price	Total

Subtotal _____
CA Residents Add 6¼% Sales Tax _____
*Postage and Handling _____
Total Amount Enclosed _____

*Postage and Handling:
$1.75 for orders under $10.00
$2.25 for orders of $10.00-$25.00
9% (max. $9.00) of order for orders over $25.00

Resource Publications, Inc.
160 E. Virginia St., #290
San Jose, CA 95112
408 286-8505   FAX 408 287-8748
☐ My check or purchase order is enclosed.
☐ Charge my: ☐Visa ☐MC Exp. Date _____
Card # _____-_____-_____-_____
Signature: _____
Name: _____
Institution: _____
Street: _____
City: _____ St.___ Zip_____
Code: GM